Accelerated Learning Bible

Advanced Learning Strategies For Unconventional Thinkers:

The Ultimate Collection To Learn Faster, Remember More And Become More Productive

Patrick Lightman

Accelerated Learning 1

Advanced Learning Strategies to Learn Faster, Remember More and be More Productive

Introduction 6

Chapter 1: What is Accelerated Learning 8

Chapter 2: Preparing to Learn 17

Chapter 3: Bringing Your A Game 23

Chapter 4: Basic Techniques to Speed Up the Learning Process 31

Chapter 5: How to Improve Your Memory and Why 44

Chapter 6: What Mistakes Really Mean 54

Chapter 7:What Mistakes Really Mean 60

Chapter 8: Preparing to Learn for Life 65

Conclusion.. 68

Accelerated Learning 2

How to learn like Einstein: Read faster, memorize more and master anything with ease - Including DIY-exercises

Introduction 71

Chapter 1: Shattering Old Paradigms 73

Chapter 2: The Keys to Effective Learning 78

Chapter 3: Setting Yourself Up For Success 82

Chapter 4: Analyze and Understand Yourself 87

Chapter 5: How to Develop Rapid Reading Skills 93

Chapter 6: How to Master the Art of Taking Smart Notes............................... 99

Chapter 7: How to Memorize Like an Elephant 105

Chapter 8: How to Properly CRAM 111

Chapter 9: Show What You Know 118

Chapter 10: Getting Things Done 123

Chapter 11: How to Get Better in Getting Better 129

Conclusion...133

Accelerated Learning 3

Learn more in less time: Direct your own education and teach yourself anything with self-learning - Including DIY-exercises

Introduction 137

Chapter 1: Why Self-Learning Beats Traditional Learning 139

Chapter 2: Principles of Self-learning 146

Chapter 3: Align Yourself for Success 152

Chapter 4: Find Your WHY 159

Chapter 5: Manage Your Outcome 167

Chapter 6: Effective Reading and Memorization 176

Chapter 7: How to Constantly Get Better in Teaching You Anything 185

Conclusion 194

Accelerated Learning

Advanced Learning Strategies to Learn Faster, Remember More and be More Productive

By Patrick Lightman

Introduction

This book contains proven steps and strategies on how to enhance your learning so you can acquire knowledge at a much faster rate.

For many people, learning in general is not easy. Many people often struggle with mastering the most basic of concepts when trying to learn something new, and muddle through school year after year with mediocre grades, and by the time they should be thinking about entering college and getting an advanced education, many have either given up or they don't care.

It doesn't help that parents, teachers, and administrators in schools buy into the old-fashioned idea cookie cutter education thus creating an endless cycle of students who are barely getting by. Fast forward all of that into a mediocre career where schools have produced class after class of students who have just lost the will to even try to learn any more.

For years, we have seen generation after generation of students lose interest in study and sad to say, it only results in a lack of interest in life in general. We are amazing creatures that have been designed to learn but when you have been mentally boxed into learning in only one approved way, one that goes against your natural grain of absorbing information, it can be very easy to give up and lose interest. Your motivation will wane and unfortunately it will affect your interest in continuing to learn in later years and by extension have a major impact on your quality of life.

However, because we have been designed to be lifelong learners, it is more important than ever that we do more when we study than just absorb information, we must also find a way to enjoy it. We live in an age where our knowledge base is constantly changing and we have to be prepared to master new things at every stage of life. It doesn't matter if you're school-aged or a senior citizen, the need to learn is directly connected to how well you can navigate the world around you and all you have to do in it.

In our modern age, new information is being released at phenomenal rates. Those who are not comfortable with not only lifelong learning but the ability to consume the information quickly will soon be left behind. This makes it more important than ever for us to embrace this new knowledge and develop a strategy that will allow us to always remain ahead of the game no matter what information is in front of us.

In the following pages of this book, we will teach you the fundamentals of accelerated learning and how to apply it in your daily lives. Together, we will learn:

- What is accelerated learning
- What you must do before you start to learn
- Basic strategies you can add to your existing study plan
- Why memory plays such an important role in learning
- How to take a negative learning experience and turn it into a positive
- And more

If you're serious about mastering new learning strategies and how you can change your world through accelerated learning, it's time to turn the page and join us on a whole new journey of learning in a whole new way. Thanks again for downloading this book, I hope you enjoy it!

Chapter 1: What is Accelerated Learning

We all need to be lifelong learners. It is key to our having a productive life and getting all the things we need to make our lives complete. Accelerated Learning is a program that basically reframes the way you've viewed learning all along. Many people are of the belief that learning is a rote exercise that involves the memorizing of long lists of facts and figures so that they can pass a test or obtain a good score however, accelerated learning is much more than that. It is a strategy that will help you to break out of that traditional line of thought opening your mind up to an endless parade of possibilities.

Once you come to a clearer understanding of what accelerated learning really is, you will be better able to set-up a more efficient environment around you, one that is more conducive to learning. You will be more effective in choosing the conditions under which you learn, one that will make it easier for your mind to absorb more information and be where you can take the new knowledge that you have acquired and extend it in practical ways that can apply to all sorts of situations in your life. In essence, accelerated learning will make you more adept at getting your brain to receive information and retain it, recalling it whenever needed in ways that will best benefit your life.

There are several fundamentals of accelerated learning that make all of this possible.

It is a means of boosting your learning power - each of us has his own way of acquiring information. When you know how to tap into your own personal learning style, learning will feel more natural to you, making it easier to acquire new knowledge, and by extension you will be able to absorb it much faster.

You will be able to tap into your five senses, which is the body's natural way of absorbing information. When you learn how to enhance your visual, auditory, and kinesthetic abilities, the information you take in will become a natural extension of yourself and the new knowledge will become more like second nature to you.

To accomplish this, there is a six-stage process to accelerated learning that has proven to be very effective. The six stages can be best remembered with the acronym M-A-S-T-E-R, which stands for:

- **M**ind set to positive:
- **A**cquire the knowledge
- **S**earch out the meaning
- **T**rigger your memory
- **E**xhibit what you know
- **R**eflect on your learning

With this type of program, the learning relies more on the doing, practicing, and applying the new knowledge rather than just reading, hearing, or seeing things. When you apply these types of techniques, you begin to enjoy your learning much more than you would otherwise.

Basically, accelerated learning is the study of how **your mind works.** Not just the study of the mind in general but because each of our minds works differently, you need to understand the mechanics of your own mind.

When you examine the brain itself, you will find amazing features that will boggle your imagination and stimulate your thinking. You may not be aware of the fact that your brain contains as many as 100 billion brain cells (or neurons) but this is not what makes your ability to learn so impressive. It is the 20,000 or so connections that are branching off from each of those neurons that make learning possible.

You don't have to be a math major in order to see the benefits of these features. Each time one of those trillions of dendrites light up, a thought occurs, a memory is formed, knowledge is acquired, and experiences are developed. Today, with all of our modern technology, scientists are actually able to see these thoughts as they occur in the brain helping us to come to a much clearer understanding of how learning happens and what works best for each of us. This understanding of how our brain works and the best way to tap into it makes up the crux of what we call accelerated learning.

Our Brain Stem

We can start by understanding the basic physiology of the brain itself. Our brain stem, the part of the brain that sits at the base of the skull and connects to the spinal column is primarily responsible for our basic life functions, those actions that we do without thinking. It controls and regulates our heart beat, our breathing, and our basic instincts. At first glance, you may not think this has anything to do with how you learn, however, once you realize that this same region of the brain is also the instinctual center of the body, you will start to see why it is so key to how we react to our external environment.

A good example of this is the instinctual flight or fight response that we all have. Think of how well you learn if you're feeling threatened or angry. When these negative emotions appear your mind literally shuts down and your only thought is to restore your consciousness to safety. When the mind senses negativity, our learning process begins to shut down but when our minds are in a more positive condition, we are more receptive to what we experience in our immediate environment and we are in a better position to receive new knowledge and retain it.

Understanding this is one of the key elements of accelerated learning. It helps us to understand just how our emotional state of mind impacts our learning. At this point, you have already learned one of the keys to mastering accelerated learning. Controlling our emotional state and making sure that we are in a positive frame of mind can automatically speed up the learning process.

Our Limbic System

Our limbic system is the part of the brain that is literally wrapped around the brain stem like a collar. There are two key components here are the hypothalamus and the amygdala. This part also plays a significant role in controlling your emotions. While the brain stem focuses on controlling instinctual emotions related to protecting your survival, the limbic system controls emotions related to your personal feelings, working constantly to keep a healthy balance within the body.

It also is responsible for the release of hormones, let's you know when you're thirsty, manages your metabolism, immune system, and your **long-term memory** (an important element in the learning process).

Your hypothalamus and amygdala are key components in managing your emotions and developing your own goal-seeking behavior. This helps us to understand why we are more inclined to respond to emotional experiences better than just plain old logical reasoning. The very fact that the same part of the brain that regulates emotions also controls our memory and since learning is completely ineffective if you can't recall it, the two must work in tandem. One without the other is fruitless. So, when you realize that the same part of the brain controls both areas you can easily see why you need to focus on them together to speed up the learning process.

If you were asked to remember your best teacher in school, chances are you can conjure up visions of one immediately. You recall what they taught you, how you felt during the lesson, and liked every detail of your time with them. Other teachers may have left vague impressions that you might struggle to recall. You remember your favorite teachers because of your positive emotional experiences you had with them. Teachers that did not connect with you on such a primal level have been easily forgotten, their names lost somewhere in the many folds of your mind.

According to many researchers, when the brain is in a positive emotional state, it releases pleasure chemicals called endorphins, which then trigger a release of a neurotransmitter called acetylcholine that literally works as a "lubricant" basically greasing the connections made between the neurons in the brain, allowing it to process new information more efficiently. This is why emotionally stimulating lessons like art, drama, music, and others are often very successful as a means of teaching new information.

The same is not true of those who experience negative emotions while studying. According to researchers reporting in the journal *Scientific American*, the limbic system acts like a switchboard connecting our senses to the brain's cortex. It analyzes each piece of new information coming in and decides whether or not it should be connected to the cortex or not. If the new information is deemed to be stressful (negative in nature) it could literally be transferred to the more primitive areas of the brain (the brain stem) where it can trigger more instinctual behavior rather than up to the cortex or the "thinking" part of the brain.

This is also the reason why before any learning period, it is important to use relaxation exercises in an attempt to reduce any negative emotions you might be experiencing before a study session.

The Neocortex

Located above the limbic brain is the neocortex. This is the very heart of your intelligence, the part of the brain that allows humans to think and process information in a way that no other creature on the planet can do. This is where your mind makes decisions, organizes your view of the world and stores any experiences you may have had. It is also the place where memory and speech are produced, where your appreciation of the arts lies, and where much of the learning happens.

The neocortex can be divided into different parts (referred to as lobes). There is a lobe dedicated to every aspect the brain must process; speech, hearing, vision, touch, taste. As we use each of our five senses, we store the memories of the data into different areas of the neocortex. If you hope to develop strong attachments to the new information you learn, it is imperative that you engage your emotional core in the process. This natural physiology of the brain is evidence that engaging your senses while learning is an important element that ensures that you can remember whatever it is you decide to learn.

Your Two Hemispheres

As you become more familiar with the three different parts of the brain, you'll also notice that the brain has two very distinct sides called the right and left hemispheres. Each of these hemispheres is responsible for different functions in the body. While both sides are connected by the corpus callous (a network consisting of approximately 300 million neurons) working as a shuttle moving information back and forth between the two hemispheres, research has shown that each side of the brain is primarily responsible for different things.

The left brain is considered to be the area where our logical thinking takes place. It is responsible for all things academic; computing mathematical processes, analyzing data and situations, sequencing information, and developing reasoning. The right brain is the more creative side of your thinking. It is where you develop your sense of rhythm, appreciation for music, visual impressions, images, color, etc. This is the part of the brain that is constantly searching for patterns, and analogies in the world around you and where you develop conceptual thoughts in relation to more abstract ideas like love, beauty, and loyalty.

While each side of the brain is primarily responsible for very specific roles, both of them are involved in the process of learning. A perfect example of this can be seen in how the brain processes a simple movement. Let's say that you are watching a red ball as it rolls along a flat surface. Your brain needs to fire up several areas of the brain in order to process what is happening. It processes the color and shape in one area, movement in another area, location in another area. In fact, four different areas of the brain must be activated for you to understand what is happening right in front of your eyes.

Yes, each hemisphere is dominant in certain elements but they are both needed to learn something well. However, if you are a person that is more left brain then your style of learning will favor the logical, more linear type of learning. You will want to be given step-by-step instructions of each part of the process but a right brain learner will want to see a more global image of the subject matter.

It is not that you only use one side of the brain or another but rather, it is finding ways of learning that appeals to your more dominant side of your brain. While both sides are active participants in the learning process, discovering which side is your dominant side and tailoring your lessons to that side will allow you to absorb information much faster than ever before.

It is a whole brain endeavor. This is why music has proven to be such a powerful way to teach lessons. When you listen to a popular song, your left brain focuses on the lyrics while the right brain is processing the melody. The limbic system is engaged in the deeper meaning of the words and tapping into your emotions. Very quickly, you will know the song and remember. Years later, you will hear just a few bars and your mind will trigger every note as if you had just heard it for the first time. This is because it engages the "whole brain" in the process. This is the core principle behind accelerated learning; it is a means of stretching your mind by engaging all facets of the brain in the learning process.

Our brains are powerful instruments and we are just now beginning to learn how to make good use of it. Most of us enjoy those activities that engage the whole brain in the thinking process because we are tapping into our emotions, our logical and reasoning abilities, as well as our creative side. We tend to lose interest however, when we are given exercises that only engage a single part of our brain. Exercises that require the memorization of long lists of information, an endless series of mathematical problems to calculate, or any type of repetitive work tends to shut down parts of our brain causing us to lose emotional attachment to the material.

The Magic Eight

Now that you understand the importance of engaging the whole brain in the learning process, it's time for you to kick your learning up another notch. The Magic Eight refers to a new way of measuring intelligence. The Theory of Multiple Intelligence, developed by

Harvard Professor Howard Gardner measures not how smart you may be based on an IQ test but rather determines how you use the intelligence you have.

His thoughts are that intelligence varies depending on the circumstances at the time and our ability to navigate them. All human beings have a unique body of skills that we rely on during varying times in our lives. We tap into those skills when we need them in ways that are unique to each of us. So, if you were stranded in the Australian outback the skills you need would be very different from those needed on the streets of New York City. Your ability to survive in each of those situations would depend on a completely different set of knowledge that you would have at your disposal.

Our intelligence therefore is our ability to manage a wide variety of problems that can range from something as basic as deciding what to wear to something that is as complicated as getting out of life or death situations. According to Gardner there are at least nine different types of intelligences we can tap into to resolve those problems. While we all have some level of each one in our repertoire, we each have several more dominant intelligences that we favor when we are trying to acquire new knowledge.

Linguistic: Linguistic Intelligence is your ability to communicate with words. You can absorb information through reading, writing, or verbally.

Logical-Mathematical: your ability to calculate figures, reason on things, or to mentally process things in a logical and systematic manner.

Visual-Spatial: Your ability to process images, visualize things in your mind's eye, and imagine future results.

Musical: your ability to create music, to compose, sing, or understand musical pieces. It also includes your ability to maintain a certain rhythm.

Bodily-Kinesthetic: your ability to use your body in variety of ways. This could involve using your hands to create products, to physically demonstrate how something is done, to present ideas in a physical manner, to express your emotions through body language.

Interpersonal: your ability to work with and interact well with others. You can relate well with others, show empathy, and understanding, and recognize other people's motivations and aspirations.

Intrapersonal: The ability to self-analyze and reflect on past experiences. To be able to sit back and analyze your past behaviors, personal feelings, and set goals based on them.

Naturalist: your ability to tap into nature and make distinctions in the natural world. To be able to identify flora and fauna in your environment and understand the basic sciences of biology.

Existential: your ability to tap into the deeper meaning of life and to connect to a higher form of existence. The ability to recognize the spiritual being that lies underneath the physical and mental person.

In traditional educational settings, the focus was always on either the linguistic or mathematical skills, which worked well for some students but for those students who weren't strong in these areas, where their natural intelligence fell into one of the other categories, they often fell through the cracks. Learning was not an emotionally stimulating experience and could prove to be extremely daunting and uncomfortable.

All of these elements make up the core of accelerated learning and give you the keys to acquiring new knowledge at a faster rate than ever before. By using these tools, you learn to tap into your own unique combination of intelligences and develop the techniques needed to use your whole brain in order to absorb the information much easier and retain it better. By doing this, you make it possible to learn much faster and get more enjoyment out of the entire process.

Chapter 2: Preparing to Learn

We've all been told that it is important to have a good learning environment to help us to learn but we never completely understood why. After decades of research though, we understand that our immediate external environment can have a significant impact on just how our brains absorb new information. But few of us think about how we can adapt our internal environment to enhance the experience of learning too.

The reality is clear, there are several factors and environmental conditions that have a direct impact on how well you learn. Once you understand these different elements and how they affect your learning, you'll be able to create the best conditions to make your learning experience easier and faster.

Your immediate environment is not just physical but can also be mental and emotional as well. Some of these things are within your ability to control them while others are not.

Your Attention Span

According to the nonprofit group Technology, Entertainment, and Design, (you're probably more familiar with it as TED Talks) most of us have a very limited attention span. Unless you're a rather exceptional individual, your ability to focus on a single topic is usually maxed out at approximately 18 minutes. When you are forced to listen to lectures that run into hours, you are losing a significant part of the lesson that may be valuable to you.

Of course, all of this is relative. You can focus more on a two-hour movie because it is passive activity. Your brain is not forced to conceptualize the information contained. Visualization work is already provided for you. On the other hand, when you are trying to absorb a lecture, you are expected to use much more brain power. You are expected to participate in open discussions, ask questions, etc. This can cause your brain to tire out and you will need a break as your mental fatigue begins to set in.

The reality is that you can only absorb information when your brain is focused. By scheduling study times that last longer than the brain is capable of absorbing information you'll find yourself spinning your wheels and losing valuable data. So, by scheduling shorter study times with regular breaks in between, you give your mind a chance to rest and process the information you've taken in before adding more on top of it.

When setting up your study schedule, factor in the periods when you tend to be the most active. Some of us are morning people and can perform well first things in the morning while others may be more night owls and can muster up more attention late at night. These are the optimum times for you to carve out study time allowing your brain to absorb more in a shorter period of time.

This does not mean that you have to limit your study time to precisely 18 minutes to be effective. Most people find success by using the 30-50-minute study sessions. If you choose a 50-minute session, you can have two 20-minute study periods with a 10-minute break in between. If you choose a 30-minute session you can have 15-minute session with a 5-minute break before another 10-minute session as a follow up.

Whatever you choose, make sure that it allows you to maximize study time without allowing you to slip into brain fatigue. Surprisingly enough, you'll find that if you follow this pattern you'll absorb more information, retain it better, and you'll enjoy studying much more than if you try to schedule in an hour long cram session.

Concepts Before Facts

Another important consideration is the order of the information you want to learn. In traditional school settings students are often inundated with long lists of facts without any practical application that allow them to mentally connect with the information they are given. According to one researcher, there are two different types of learning. There is the surface and the deep learning styles.

With surface learning, you are able to accumulate entire lists of facts to memorize whereas with deep learning your mind focuses on the abstract meaning of the subject and how it applies to reality. You might conclude that deep learning is more important but in reality, there is a time and place for both types of learning.

When your study is focused entirely on memorization, your brain starts to isolate single pieces of information without any way of relating them to a particular concept. There is nothing anchoring them in your mind, however, when you are given them in a context situation you can start to identify connections, patterns, and relationships between the information then your brain has something to hold onto.

The ability to identify patterns is what makes learning useful, otherwise the information you've learned has no useful purpose that makes the mind want to hold onto them. If you can find that underlying pattern (right brain activity) or concept and follow it through to a logical conclusion you would be able to determine the relatability and will make a more personal connection to it.

For example, suppose you are studying the Miranda rights in your history class. With surface learning, you would learn the names of the Supreme Court Justices, the lawyers that argued the case, and the names of all the other parties that were involved. You may even remember the exact date the case was heard, the number of votes and how many appeals it had leading up to the case.

But while all of these facts have a bearing on the subject, they don't connect you to the information you're taking in. They mean nothing to you, they are just lists of information. However, if you wanted to look more deeply at the subject you would search out the underlying concept that surrounds the reason for this information, then when you did come across the facts relating to the case, they would be much easier to remember. So, concepts allow you to give the specific facts and details involving the subject a home base in your brain, giving you a personal connection to the case and how it relates to you and your life today. You would learn about the rights of the defendants and how they have evolved and can affect you today.

As you master this skill of concept learning you will learn how to categorize different facts by the specific attributes, identify patterns, and integrate them into your mind in a way that will help you to recall them later.

This technique can be applied to more than just school and book learning. It can be used to develop new skills all throughout life and as a result give more meaning to your life in general. It helps you to understand the main point of each new thing you learn, not just the facts surrounding it. When you are looking for new information, look for more than just "what" happened, look for the "why" as well. It is the "why" that will give you the concept behind everything you learn.

Your Frustration Level

Being an accelerated learner does not in any way imply that you will master everything right the first time. In fact, the truth is just the opposite. You will fail and fail often, especially when you are trying to master a new skill. In accelerated learning, this is referred to as "Productive Failure," a term coined by Manu Kapur, a researcher at the National Institute of Education in Singapore. His theory lies in the fact that if you give a student a reliable model to learn from, continuing guidance and support, and maintain it until they master their skill it is a key secret to success. As a result of supplying them with a safe place to test out their new theories, they will flounder again and again, learning and mastering a little more of the skill until they reach a point of full mastery.

It is the basis of all learning experiences we have as a child. When we are born, we come with a completely blank slate. We do not know how to talk, walk, play, interact, or even take care of our basic needs. However, it is through trial and error that we slowly master all of these skills and master them to the point that they become second nature to us. We learn to walk by repeatedly falling and pulling ourselves back up, we learn to speak by constantly making sounds, mimicking the sounds we hear from others around us until we actually form words.

At some point, we start to view failure as something bad and something to be ashamed of and it is at this point that we start to flounder in our learning. We lose our confidence and begin to see learning as a chore rather than a natural life experience. However, it has been shown through several research studies, that the ability to learn how to solve problems comes from those failed experiences that we are so reluctant to have. When we attempt something and fail at it, our minds have to work towards figuring out what went wrong and then trying several attempts at the problem until we get it right. By avoiding the "mistakes" we are actually restricting our ability to learn and grow.

With each failure, you learn more about the specific problem and can use that knowledge more effectively the next time you attempt to find a solution. According to Kapur, there are three different factors that make embracing failure an effective learning tool.

1. It allows you to work on problems that offer a challenge
2. It provides you with the opportunity to explain and detail the steps in your process
3. It allows you to make comparisons and contrasts for both good and bad solutions

As a result, with each attempt to solve a problem and each successive failure, you reinforce the knowledge you have, correct wrong conclusions, and refine the learning process all at the same time. Sad to say, at some point, society and educators in general have reached the conclusion that the end result is what's important and not the process it took to get there. By embracing your failures, the ability to work out problems becomes the primary concern and students are less reluctant to hide their mistakes allowing everyone to address the weak areas in learning, making it faster and more efficient.

The key here is to control your level of frustration that is often associated with failure. By viewing these mistakes as stepping stones rather than a blight on your character, you can develop a strategy that will help to solve the problem in a more productive way allowing you to learn from your experiences rather than to allow them to deflate you and diminish your self-confidence.

You must be realistic here. After repeated attempts to solve a problem, you will eventually feel frustration and at times have to fight of the temptation to quit. If you allow those feelings to overtake you, it could lead to excessive anxiety that will eventually impact your studies. But if you expect this type of frustration ahead of time, you can develop a plan to respond to it in a more positive way. More often than not, when frustration levels get high, it may be best to take a break from the problem and allow your brain a chance to recover. Focus your attention on something else for a while and when you come back to it, you'll see the problem through fresh eyes, with less anxiety associated with it. Often when you have a more relaxed frame of mind to work with, the answers flow much more easily than if you are under stress.

So, while preparing your immediate external environment to create an atmosphere that is more conducive to study, knowing how to prepare mentally for study is equally if not more important. So often, people delve into the depths of study without understanding their own psychological and emotional make-up, or even knowing how their own brain works and as a result, create an environment that could turn out to be hit or miss for the learning experience. By preparing yourself mentally, understanding your limitations, and working within the confines of your own ability, you avoid spinning your wheels in the study process and open yourself up to an unlimited potential that will accelerate your learning in many ways.

Chapter 3: Bringing Your A Game

As we have already learned, when you know how the brain works it makes it much easier to accumulate new information. There are some very specific strategies that will help you to accelerate your learning by bringing your A game to the table.

Let's go back to what we have already come to understand about the brain and how it works. We've already discussed that when you learn something new, you create a connection in one of the trillions of connections. Each new piece of knowledge you acquire is stored in a specific neuron in your brain. It arrives at that particular neuron via connections called dendrites. Learning is the process of creating new connections for each new piece of information you pick up.

A good example of this is when you meet someone. Let's say his name is Alfred. Once you have that knowledge, there is a neuron set aside for your knowledge of Alfred. If when you meet him, you see his face, there is a dendrite connection created that plants a visual image of Alfred in your brain. If you shook his hand, you now have a textile memory of him created in a new dendrite. If you noticed his smile, listened to his voice, noticed his after shave, or even engaged in a little banter, you create a new dendrite in the brain for each piece of new information about him. The more connections you create, the easier it will be to recall this valuable information at a later time.

As you can see, it is not enough to want to learn and to be motivated, you also need to bring your many other elements into play with every bit of detail you hope to learn.

One of the most unfortunate things about traditional learning is that it is often presented too much by rote. The idea of teachers spewing out information in a singular fashion and students being expected to parrot it back to them in a certain order has removed much of the imagination from the entire experience.

To accomplish this, you must be willing to go beyond the books and the calculators to enhance your learning. One would be purely amazed at the power a few simple exercises can have "before" the learning begins. Once applied and put to the test, your whole body will be prepared to engage in learning without hesitation and in fact, will be looking forward to it with a great deal of anticipation.

All of this starts with just a little creative thinking. It starts with the ability to visualize your success at tackling the more difficult subjects before you begin to study. This will frame your mind in such a way that it will boost your motivation and confidence in the subject you are about to undertake. Already, around the globe, this is a practice that has been put in place with many world-class athletes. But this skill does not have to be limited to those in the athletic arena. Whether you're doing scientific research, preparing for a business meeting, or you're just looking for a solid political standing, your ability to envision the end goal before you start will be extremely successful in mentally preparing you for the lessons you hope to master.

This brings us to one key element when it comes to learning. It requires some personal reflection about the act of learning itself. Motivation - or the belief that you really do want to learn can make a huge difference in bringing your "A Game" to the experience. When you are not motivated, commitment to follow through on the lessons is often weak, if not non-existent. A lack of motivation or a desire to master the topic you're trying to absorb could close your mind off from any type of learning experience.

To determine your personal level of motivation, you need to do a little personal introspection. Whether you're trying to master a new skill, tackle a new subject, or just improve your already existing knowledge, your personal investment in the task will weigh heavily on whether or not you will succeed. If you are reluctant, have developed a negative attitude about it, or are in any way unreceptive to the lesson, you are more inclined to view it as a burdensome chore and inevitably setting yourself up for failure.

This does not mean that you won't have some negative feelings. Any time you tackle anything new, doubts, fears, and anxieties are just a natural part of it. After all, you're about to embark on a whole new territory where you will most likely start out navigating unfamiliar terrain, but your level of motivation is the single most important key to helping you to overcome them.

You will have to make an active choice to push aside those negative feelings and change them for more positive viewpoints. Remember, the more actively engaged in the process you are the better you'll be able to learn. This is a factor that you can control.

Know Your Why

No matter what new endeavor you hope to undertake, it is more important than ever that you understand why you are doing it. This is just as important when it comes to learning. Ask yourself, what you hope to gain from learning this new information. You have to visualize a positive end result in order to be successful and get started on the right track.

There are probably many reasons why you may have chosen to take on the subject you're trying to master. Perhaps you want to get a promotion on your job, maybe you're looking to master a new skill or talent, or you need to keep up a specific GPA in order to get into the university you plan to attend. Since we all study for different reasons, we will have very different reasons for wanting to learn something new. Just make sure that your why is something strong enough to motivate you to tackle the steps and techniques we will be learning later on in this book.

It will pay off in a big way if you take the time to ask realistic questions and search out your reason for tackling your particular topic. And don't be embarrassed by your answers, it can be quite cathartic to honestly appraise your inner motivations in helping you to achieve your goals. So, if you're truly not interested in studying Quantum Physics in your university class and the only reason you signed up was because of that cute guy in the front row, it helps to understand that from the very beginning.

Whatever the reason, your motivation has to be strong enough to boost your desire to learn. This means that you must search out the benefits you will gain and be able to visualize yourself achieving them before you start. This requires a strong sense of imagination as you do this. Our imagination is an extremely powerful weapon and being able to harness it and use it to move us to advance towards our goals could be the most valuable weapon you have in your arsenal.

Once you've identified your "why" then you need to play a game of Mind Switch. Think of this like driving a car. You may have a good engine, fuel in the tank, oil, and everything you need to move the car where you need to go but if you're not able to put it in gear, then no matter what you want, the car is not going to move, period.

So, once you know your why, you then need to start getting your whole body prepared to engage in the learning process. Start by doing some simple breathing exercises. Take in a few deep breaths, filling your lungs with air, then take a long, slow exhale, pushing your stomach out as you do. Relax your neck and jaw muscles (this is the area of the body that tends to hold the most tension).

Finally, set the environment by playing some relaxing music, something that will help to put you into the right frame of mind. We've already learned that the brain is an incredible learning machine but it can only function well when it is in a relaxed state. As soon as you begin to introduce stress into the equation, it is almost as if you've wiped your mind clean. Before you attempt to study anything on your subject, it is very important that you make sure that you are in a relaxed state mentally.

To mentally relax before your lesson, try doing a few visualization exercises. It is one thing to have a goal that you are working for and it is another thing entirely to believe that you will master that goal. This is where visualization comes in. Take the time to see your success in mastering your subject in your mind's eye. This is much easier if you know how to engage all of your senses in this exercise.

See yourself completing your lesson and mastering the task you are trying to learn
Feel the sense of satisfaction and pride in knowing that you have accomplished your goal
Hear the comments of praise and recognition you will receive from other people

The more you are able to engage the senses, the easier it will be for you to see your success before you ever start your first lesson. This method of mental preparation works as a cocoon that will insulate you from external negativity in your environment. The more relaxed you are the easier it will be to shut out the craziness and chaos in the world around you so you can concentrate more on your lessons.

This works even better if you are able to find a place where you can shut the world out and completely isolate yourself from all things external. If you have a quiet place to create your own physical environment you will do much better. There you can create a pleasing visual atmosphere, add in the kind of music that is soothing to your soul, and even enhance it with essential oils, giving you the kind of fragrances that you enjoy. Adding a few plants, artwork, or just letting the natural sunlight stream in can do wonders for mentally getting you ready to study.

Becoming successful when it comes to study is really a mental game. Your mind is an interesting anomaly. You need to use brain power to learn but just like any other tool, you need to know how to use it to your advantage in order to get the best out of it. One way to do this is through positive affirmations.

By repeating out loud positive things about yourself, eventually your mind will begin to believe that your goals are possible and will start working to help you achieve them. For example, making the expression "I am confident about learning" even when you believe internally that the task is huge, will build up the motivation you need to succeed. The key here is to make sure that your expressions are positive enough. For example, rather than making statements like..."I wish I were more confident" try saying "I feel confident and sure that I can accomplish this task." Simply make the statement as if it were already true and eventually, the mind will accept it and give you exactly what you need to succeed.

Don't try to over complicate this step. In fact, it works best if you keep your affirmations positive and simple. They are far easier to remember and are more likely to be successful. Don't be shy about doing this. Some people feel as if they must appear crazy to others. Imagine the looks you get if you are walking down the street, talking to yourself before a class or before your study session. Still, try to avoid this type of thinking. After all, most of us are exposed to negative comments for the better part of our lives, if we balance the scales with a few positive ones, we are much more likely to succeed and become a successful learner than if we let the negativity from others enter into our world.

Make it a habit to repeat your affirmations whenever possible and even more often when you are faced with a particular challenge during your studies. As you say them, try to bring in visualization by imagining yourself actually accomplishing your goals and benefiting from them.

Your Goals

One very important element to successful learning is that you need to know exactly what you're aiming for. You already know that you want to master a specific task or achieve a certain goal but if that is all you do, it will be difficult to find success. When you are setting your goals for each session, you need to delve a little deeper into what you want to accomplish.

This is where you want to refine your goals and create a plan of action that will help you to get there. It is not enough for you to set out to cover a set number of pages during each study session. While that may be a target you want to reach it does not feed into your goals successfully. To be successful, you need to have a clear view of what your study session hopes to achieve and believe that you can successfully achieve it.

According to a study of several peak performers and successful people, it revealed that they all had an above-average ability to use their imagination and visualization to create a plan of action. In fact, they all had one specific thing in common. They started every task with a very clear picture of what they wanted to accomplish at the end.

This type of imagery involves not just conjuring up pictures of success in your mind but will require you to engage all of your senses. When you are creating your end goal, you should not only see the images you want but also hear the sounds, feel the sensations, and even smell or taste the elements in your picture. Needless to say, this is a very deep and profound type of imagery that once mastered, can prove to be one of the most effective learning tools in your arsenal.

This technique works because as impressive as the brain can be, it does not have the ability to distinguish between an actual event and one that has been created. It will use the same electrochemical pathways to process both. So, if you can create a positive enough visual image of your goal, your brain will believe it and will accept it as real, making it possible for you to accomplish your goals.

A perfect example of this can be easily illustrated with an exercise. Imagine you are in your home and you are about to make lemonade. You have chosen several large but firm lemons. In your mind, pick one up and feel its dimpled surface. It is firm and slightly heavy for its small size. Raise the lemon to your nose and inhale its strong scent of citrus.

Now, with a sharp knife, cut the lemon in half. As the knife slices through it, notice the light spray of juice as a few tiny drops break free from the skin and permeates the air. The inner skin is in direct contrast with the pale yellow color of the juice as it gently flows out. Now, the smell is a little stronger than before.

Raise one half of the lemon to your mouth and take a big bite, letting the juices bathe the inside of your mouth before swallowing. Taste the sourness of it.

As you perform this type of imagery, notice what is happening in real life. Chances are your mouth is watering a little as you taste the sourness of the lemon. Maybe you squinted up your lips and you might have even winced a little as you thought about how it tastes. But none of this is actually real yet your body responded just the same.

What you have experienced is something we call synesthesia. In your mind, you created the feel, the sight, the smell, and the taste and your brain responded to it as if you were really doing these things. It triggered the salivary glands in your mouth and told them to cleanse your palate of the sour taste. Even reading this book (or any other book) is a form of synesthesia. The words are not real but they are designed to lead you to create an image in your mind, which directly controls what your actions will be.

By applying this type of imagery to your studies, it send s powerful message to your subconscious that tells you that what you are reading, imagining, or creating is actually real. Not only will this help you to develop powerful tools to accelerate your learning but it will also make learning an experience you are not likely to forget.

After putting yourself in the proper state of mind to study, you will create an atmosphere that will not only relieve much of the stress associated with study but will also give you a certain level of confidence in the belief that you can succeed in reaching your goals. This is often referred to as a "resourceful" frame of mind because it gives your brain several positive resources from which it can call upon when the study becomes challenging.

You have just given yourself the first of several key strategies to help you get ready to learn. Preparing your mind to a more positive mental state that is ready to learn. The next chapter will give you five more techniques that will help you to succeed as an accelerated learner. They are simple, free, and practical to use and are in a form that no other person could rob you of. We may not have the power to change our external environment and what happens around us, but we do have the power to control what goes into our mind and how it influences our behavior. With these tools at our disposal, we are ready to bring our A game into the study process and in the end, we will learn in a way that we never could have before.

Chapter 4: Basic Techniques to Speed Up the Learning Process

Now that you have mentally prepared for the study, you are ready to jump into the accelerated learning techniques that will prove to be even more effective. When you read the words, accelerated learning you are likely thinking that it involves simply learning faster but there is much more involved than that.

Many people are of the belief that accelerated learning means you will read over material one time, remember it and use it from then on. While elements of that thought may be true, accelerated learning does not mean that you won't' have to study; it does not mean that we can simply open up your mind, pour in the knowledge and it will be stored in perpetuity. You will still have to study, you will still have to put for the effort to acquire the knowledge you are trying to achieve. However, if you apply the techniques we are about to discuss, you will learn the information with less stress and anxiety, and you will feel more satisfied with the results you achieve. You will feel confident about what you learn and you will not feel overwhelmed even when trying to master more complicated topics.

The techniques to actually apply to the learning process are the key components to helping you acquire knowledge faster and the way they are applied are the primary reason why you will be able to recall that new knowledge when you need it. There are six different techniques involved in mastering accelerated learning. We've already discussed the first one, now let's look at the other five.

Strategy #2 Acquire the Information

As we've already discussed, everyone of us has a unique composite of learning styles so the way one person will acquire new knowledge is not the way another person would. You may be primarily a kinesthetic learner where you have to learn by doing things, touching things, and actively participating in any type of exercise in order to learn where another student may simply be able to master the knowledge simply by reading the material in front of them.

It is always a good idea to sit down and figure out exactly what method of learning works best for you. Some people learn when they are left alone to figure things out while others may need the guidance of a teacher hovering over them. Some may require a perfectly tidy work area where someone else may need a little chaos.

Whatever your preferences, when you are ready to acquire knowledge there is one thing that you will need to keep in mind. Your learning experience must be active and not passive. The more you are engaged in the activity of acquiring knowledge the easier ti will be to absorb the information. It is not enough to sit by and passively listen to a lecture or superficially engage in reading. Even if you are involved in a reading exercise it does not need to be passive. As you read, consider asking yourself questions or applying the information you are reading in some way.

The more sensory involvement you can engage in the faster you will learn. It is your responsibility to make sure that you are taking in the information in a way that will benefit you. As long as you are comfortable and relaxed in how you choose to take in the information, you will be able to absorb it more easily. There are several different approaches that can make that happen.

1. Look for the main idea first. Get a good overview of the project and try to understand it. The easiest way to do this is by looking at the chapter titles and subheadings first. Rather than read your text in a chronological order, by first flipping through the subheadings and titles, you get the general idea of each lesson. Take the time to look at any images or illustrations that are there. This way, you have the basic idea down before you start to delve into the specifics.

2. Next you want to determine what is the main point of the lesson. This is key to getting a good understanding of what the purpose of the text is about. What is the point of the text, it's purpose, and how you can expect to benefit from it. Once you understand these elements, not only does the entire subject become more interesting, you are more likely to remember it for a longer period of time.

3. Take notes. Whether you will have the time or the desire later on to review them or not, the act of taking notes introduces another of your senses into the learning process. It adds the kinesthetic or bodily function to enhance and reinforce what you are learning.

   1. Start by writing down everything you already know about the subject. This will help to boost your self confidence. You will begin to realize that you have some knowledge of the subject but it will also allow you to see exactly what areas you need to more knowledge in. By doing this you will be able to to zero in on your weak areas rather than use the session as a sporadic review of what you have already learned.

   2. Take additional notes on areas you want to learn more about.

   3. Create questions

   4. Start an active search for the answers.

4. Divide the work into small bites. There is no doubt that tackling a huge textbook can be daunting, some of them can be hundreds of pages long. If it is a new topic or field of interest it can feel very intimidating. But if you take the time to divide the text up into smaller sessions, then you are less likely to be discouraged and end up giving up even before you get started. By breaking the material up into smaller bite-sized study sessions, you can ensure that you will accomplish small successes without getting overwhelmed keeping your motivation and confidence in tact.

5. Ask questions. As you go through the lesson, continue to ask questions and then search for the answers. These are the facts and details that you will be most likely remember when needed. The act of asking questions is a means of keeping your mind focused on the topic. Of course there are many questions that could be asked about a subject but as a general rule, always make sure that you have the answers to the 5 Ws; who, what, when, where, and why. Who will tell you who's involved, what will identify its meaning and purpose, when will give you a time frame, where will reveal the location, and why

will answer its purpose. You could also ask the all-important How as well, which will tell you exactly how you can use the information and what affect it will have on your overall life in general.

Apply the Three Core Activities

Sometimes referred to as the VAK attack, this is when you apply the three most powerful elements of learning: Visual, Auditory, and Kinesthetic. This goes to the core of accelerated learning. We all absorb new information in completely different ways. These are the three primary ways we receive information. Learning through observation, hearing, and activities. While we all use all three ways to receive information, the majority of us have one that we prefer to rely on more. According to recent studies the percentages seem to be nearly equal when we are young with 29% preferring to receive information visually, 34% preferring auditory, and 37% with a strong preference towards kinesthetic.

However, studies also show that as we get older or preferences began to change with more people preferring visual learning over the other two. While we don't really know the reason behind this shift, some researchers point out that as much as 70% of our human body's sensory receptors are located in our eyes. In fact, in order for the retina of the eye to absorb light rays, it holds 120 million Rods and 7 million cones. Each of these rods and cones are designed to focus on a single tiny spec within our field of vision.

Keeping that thought in mind, studies performed at the University of Wisconsin have shown that when visual aids are used in learning, students experienced as much as 200% improvement in retention. Simply by adding visual aids to your study regimen will allow you to absorb the information must faster and easier.

To apply the VAK attack, you will have to approach the way you take in new information differently. You will have to start looking for things that are not explicitly spoken, listen for things that are not so blatantly heard, and feel things you've never felt before. You'll be looking under the surface for elements of the material that are not so easily seen.

While you may be able to absorb information in all three areas, it helps immensely when you know exactly which one of the three is your personal preference. That way, if you use study styles that incorporate your dominant sensory preference, you will capitalize on your strong suits and make your study time much more efficient.

Strategy #3 - Search Out the Meaning

We've said it before. In order for you to get the most out of a lesson or study session, it is important that you understand and can relate to it on a personal level. For this to happen, you need to focus on not just learning facts but on understanding the meaning of the lesson. When studying, the true meaning of a topic may not be readily seen and will require you to a) ask questions or b) look underneath the surface for more information.

To fully search out the meaning of something, it may be necessary to apply several different intelligences. Each one of us has at least nine possible ways to explore a topic in order to fully grasp the meaning behind any subject you choose to learn. By utilizing them in the right way you can fully create a learning style that takes advantage of your strengths and helps you to grow in knowledge.

By finding ways to use as many of these intelligences as possible it will trigger the mind to start thinking in totally different ways. A natural byproduct of this type of talent is that you will become more creative and innovative in your approach to many different things. Explore alternative options of study that go beyond the traditional school setting, which is primarily focused on logical and sequential presentation of a subject. However, when you engage in a topic that accesses all eight intelligences, you have a much better chance of hitting on one method that will be more efficient in teaching you the underlying meaning of a subject.

Finding Your Preferred Intelligence

Since we all have a unique collection of intelligences, you may find that you have more than one you rely on. Also, our battery of intelligence changes over the years. As we've already discussed, those who are younger get much more out of a kinesthetic and participatory form of study while those who are older prefer a more visual approach. Still, at any given time in your life, one and possible more forms will be your preferred method.

Linguistic: Those who are linguistically inclined enjoy playing word games, tongue-twisters, poetry, and stories. They are voracious readers willing to read everything in sight if given the opportunity. They are comfortable expressing themselves orally or in written form, and are very good storytellers. They usually have a strong vocabulary and are often asked to explain certain words they may use in conversation.

Logical-Mathematical: If you love working with numbers and can perform mathematical computations in your head, then you're probably strong in this area. People who are keenly interested in progressive advancements in science and enjoy experimenting with different things would also fall into this category. People who can balance their checkbook with ease, manage a budget, and enjoy extensively detailed vacations or business trips are also strong in logical mathematical intelligence. They enjoy brain teasers and puzzles and are quick to point out flaws in the logic of others around them.

Visual-Spatial: Those who appreciate the visual arts including paintings, sculpture, or drawing will be strong in this area of intelligence. They are excellent at keeping visual records of events by taking lots of pictures and videos. When idle, they enjoy doodling or taking notes on things they see around them. They can read a map easily and navigate the highways without problem. They are skilled at taking things apart just to see how they work.

Bodily-Kinesthetic: These are people who love sports and physical exercise. They enjoy taking walks, swimming, and the feeling they get after a really good workout. These are the type of people that need to physically handle something in order to understand it. They need the feel of the object between their fingers, to manipulate it, and maneuver it. They enjoy working on jigsaw puzzles or making things with their hands.

Musical: Those with musical intelligence are able to play some type of musical instrument, many are capable of singing - on key, and they are very adept at remembering a tune even if they have only heard it a few times. They prefer to listen to music wherever they are and enjoy attending musical events like concerts, plays, or symphonies. They have a good sense of rhythm and they find it difficult to imagine a life without some type of music as a big part of it. For them, music can easily trigger a wide range o emotions and visual imagery.

Interpersonal: These are people who enjoy working with others. They are excellent team players and enjoy being a part of a group or a committee. They make excellent mentors and advisors to others and because of that many seek them out for help in all sorts of problems. They prefer team activities like sports and games and are very social. They are excellent communicators and have no problem stepping up to the plate when something needs to be done.

Intrapersonal: These tend to be very introverted, preferring to spend more of their time with themselves. They enjoy solitude where they can reflect on the more important issues of life. They are independent and know their own mind. Many have their own hobbies or work that they prefer to do alone and enjoy sports like fishing and hiking, content with their own company. Intrapersonal people know themselves very well, clear on both their weaknesses and their strengths and prefer working for themselves rather than working for other people.

Naturalist: Those who are naturalists get the most enjoyment out of nature. They can easily recognize flora and fauna in their locale and have a keen interest in understanding how nature works in general. If given the opportunity, they can track wildlife, read the weather signs, and can visualize themselves in a natural climate. They love gardening, are concerned about the environment, and some have extended their interest in nature to the stars.

Existentialists: The newest of all the multiple intelligences is sometimes referred to as spiritual intelligence. These are people who are not afraid to examine the bigger and deeper meaning to life. They are highly sensitive to conceptualizing about the meaning of life and the purpose of our own human existence. They have a sense of cosmic wonder or a spiritual awareness that transcends much of what most people would consider in depth contemplation. These people tend to have what some might refer to as a sixth sense about the world around them, they are highly insightful, and some have even been described as having psychic abilities.

By applying each of your strong intelligences to your study, you literally become able to bring the information to life. It will become more memorable allowing you to interpret facts and examine them in their true nature. You can draw conclusions, do comparisons, and evaluate the importance of what you are learning and make it meaningful to you.

Keep in mind that your entire purpose for using these intelligences is to help you to not only absorb new knowledge but to find the meaning behind the information. This will give you a deeper understanding of what you are learning and find ways that can help you to relate to it on a more personal level.

Strategy #4 Activate Your Memory

The third step in the learning process is to activate your memory. You've probably already heard of those people who have what seems to be an infallible memory. They can recall details of events that may have happened years ago with amazing clarity. They have perfect recall.

After years of study of these people, scientists have been unable to uncover any distinguishable difference between the brains of these people and the brains of the average person. This leads us to believe that it is not that they have a unique mental ability but more a matter of how they use the same tools that we all have.

Activating your memory is merely a matter of applying several strategies that can help to lock the information into your long-term memory banks. There are three fundamental strategies that we have already talked about that will allow you to do this.

1. Put yourself in the right frame of mind before you begin studying
2. Find new ways to absorb the information that taps into your natural way of learning
3. Take the time to search out the deeper meaning of the information and apply it on a more personal level.

In all of those studies conducted on those with perfect recall, one thing did become very clear to researchers. Approximately 70% of new information you learn will be completely forgotten within a single 24-hour period if you do not take the necessary steps to store it in your long-term memory.

It is important to note that all people do not have the same ability to remember. Just like they have different strengths when it comes to intelligence, they also have different types of memories. Some people are better at remembering faces, others numbers, and others perhaps can remember names well. Very few people have the mastery over all aspects of memory. Still, everyone can improve their memory with the right strategies applied.

The key here is in how you introduce the new information into your mind. Our brain will automatically sift through information and does not pay much attention to the usual things. However, it will focus on those things that are unusual in nature. This is because our minds will automatically gravitate to those things that are odd, bizarre, funny, and even behaviors or conversations that fall outside of what is considered to be normal human conduct. So, you are more likely to remember that rude person in the supermarket than the polite cashier that you see every day.

The brain also naturally latches on to order. Even without realizing it, we group things together. Whether it is animals, scenes from nature, or simply your grocery list, even the most disorganized person has some level of mental order he needs to maintain. By organizing your material into categories, your brain will be more receptive to it because it engages you on an active level. You are creating associations between the different elements of the lesson and it will be easier to remember.

Making those associations is very important because your mind is like a vault used to store valuable knowledge. Think of all the millions of pieces of knowledge you have accumulated throughout your life. If there was no order to your mind, it would be literally impossible for you to retrieve any information when you needed it. With each passing day, you are accumulating and adding even more knowledge to your mind complicating the retrieval process even more.

But if you have an order to the information, language stored in one part of the brain, numbers in another, visual images in another, and in another place mathematical calculations and so on it will be much easier to find and retrieve the information you need. When there is an order to how to absorb your information, recalling it later will be much easier and definitely faster.

Of course, there are many different techniques you can use to trigger your memory so feel free to design your own memory aid. Remember your brain is unique and only you know exactly what works best for you. Just keep in mind that the key to triggering the memory is in how you acquire the information.

Once you believe you have successfully absorbed the information, give your brain time to register it and record it in its proper place. Often we forget things simply because we fail to perform this one step. Several studies have now shown that when you give your mind a rest, it allows the brain to actually file away any new information you've acquired into its proper place. This usually happens during the REM stage when you are sleeping, so make sure that you give your mind enough rest to ensure that you will recall it when you need it later on.

While this aspect of the brain is yet to be fully understood, research has shown that a simple three step process ensures that your new knowledge is firmly planted in the brain so that it can easily be recalled later.

1. Acquire the knowledge

2. Review the information just before going to sleep

3. Review the information again when you wake up

Strategy #5 Demonstrate Your New Knowledge

For years, parents have diligently asked their children the same question every day when they returned home from school. What did you learn today? The question seemed simple enough and for the parents it was simply a gauge to determine if their child was performing well in school. But now, as we come to understand how our brain works, we are realizing that this step has been very important in helping us to reinforce what we learned, literally locking in the lesson in our minds.

Demonstrating knowledge has powerful yet practical implications for anyone interested in accelerating their learning. It gives you the chance to apply your new knowledge in more meaningful ways and it helps you to see if you have any weak areas where you might have to work a little more to fill in the gaps.

If you have applied the first four strategies well, then you can consider this step a kind of test that will allow you to prove to yourself that you have truly learned the new material. To make sure that you really understand it and have the information locked in, you want to be able to recreate it in a different form.

Depending on what you have learned, there are a myriad different ways that you can demonstrate your new knowledge. Whatever you choose, make sure that you try to incorporate a variety of intelligences into the project. Some people prefer some of these suggestions:

• Review using flash cards

• Create a visual image of the new information

• Create tables, graphs, flow charts, etc.

- Make a list placing each element in order
- Repeat it back to themselves
- Explain it to someone else

Your choice of which technique to use will depend largely on your preferred learning style and the primary intelligences you utilize. Whatever method you choose, make sure that you look for errors in your conclusions, holes in your understanding, and weaknesses in your ability to demonstrate the knowledge. These are issues that should be addressed in your next study session.

Strategy # 6 Reflect on What You've Learned

Similar to the previous step, the final stage of accelerated learning is to take the time to reflect on what you have learned. This is the time to review and evaluate what new knowledge you have acquired and just how you plan to apply it in the future. This is when you take ownership of your new knowledge and find practical applications where you can.

One of the reasons people tend to forget so easily is because few rarely take the time to execute this step. However, self-analysis is the key to successful learning. While it may require taking the time to reflect on the material in a meaningful way, without this type of evaluation, your rewards will be limited.

It goes to understanding that your brain can only latch onto something if you're conscious of it. This point can't be emphasized enough. As a matter of fact, a research associate at the Harvard Graduate School of Education, David Perkins, has actively argued that there should actually be a tenth intelligence called "Reflective Intelligence" that we all must possess to some degree. He points out that not only do traditional schools fail to encourage this step in the learning process, those who do manage to develop the skill usually have to do so on their own.

Reflecting on a personal learning experience is important for everyone, regardless to whether they **are in school or not. Reflection can be done in a variety of ways including writing in journals, creating charts, or in open discussions with**

others. When done well, it encourages the development of intrapersonal intelligence allowing the student to learn more about their own strengths and weaknesses.

If you're not accustomed to doing reflection exercises, it may be difficult at first but by asking some very basic questions, you can easily get your mind thinking in the right direction.

1. What went well
2. What could I have done better
3. How can I improve the next time

Once you learn to do an honest appraisal of yourself then you'll be able to fine tune your learning sessions, literally tailoring them to meet your unique and specific needs no matter what you plan to study.

Chapter 5: How to Improve Your Memory and Why

There is a lot involved in learning how to learn. We've already discussed how understanding how your brain works and how your emotions impact your thought process when it comes to taking in new knowledge. However, we have only scratched the surface when it comes to true learning. Yes, all of the things we've discussed are of the utmost importance before you begin your course of study, but there is one more essential element that will be absolutely necessary in creating the right learning environment. That is your memory.

Without a good functioning memory, your ability to learn will only benefit you temporarily because as soon as you've stepped out of the learning environment, all your new knowledge will simply evaporate and will be of no lasting benefit to you. The fact is that you cannot bring your A Game to the table if you don't have any way of storing the new knowledge you acquire.

In order to get the most out of your study session, it will help immensely if you understand how your memory actually works, eventually that positive viewpoint will override these internal feelings and you will begin to believe them.

At this point, let's clarify what we're talking about here when we say memory. We're not talking about the mundane task of memorizing long lists of words, facts, or phrases that are often assigned in traditional classroom settings. Memory in this context is your ability to store information in your brain in a way that makes it easy to retrieve when you need it in the future. There are three basic steps to creating a memory:

1. Encoding
2. Storage
3. Retrieval

If any one of these steps is not executed properly, the information you achieve could be lost somewhere in your brain only to reappear at the wrong time. When you cannot retrieve it when needed, then the whole process of learning becomes moot.

Encoding: As you learn information, your brain needs to process all of the data that it receives from your senses. You may not be aware of it but your brain is constantly at work sifting through all of the information and coding it either in your conscious or your subconscious mind. This is a very important fact to help you to remember details better.

There are several factors that determine exactly if and where your brain will store all your information.

1. The amount of attention you giving this new information
2. Your motivation or desire to know it
3. Your emotional and psychological state
4. The number of distractions....

If you are devoted to the lesson and giving it the needed attention then your brain will work harder to store the information in a place where you can access it later. However, if you are distracted, watching a movie at the same time, or otherwise uninterested in the topic, the brain may store the information in your short-term memory banks. But it will require a special combination of requirements to be met for that data to pass through the gate and find its way to your long-term memory, the most treasured place in the mind.

Storage: After the information is encoded, the brain then must decide where it will be go. Think of it like a massive file cabinet and the new information is a file that needs to be put away. There are three different types of memory storage systems you need to know about.

1. Sensory
2. Short-term
3. Long-term

Sensory memory is the shortest of the three. These thoughts are stored just long enough so they can be transferred to your short-term memory if needed. It allows information collected by your five senses to be held in place for a short time after the original stimulus is no longer present. A good example of sensory memory is when you get a glimpse of something before it completely disappears from view. For a few moments after the view of it has faded, the brain will continue to hold its impression for.. There are two primary forms of sensory memory, iconic or visual memory and echoic or audio memory.

Retrieval: the final step of creating a memory is the retrieval phase, which is what we are often referring to when we recall something to mind. The brain retrieves stored memories in different ways. There are some things you will be able to remember without any specific trigger and there are other memories that will require a cue to bring them up. Other memories may only be recalled in a particular sequence or as a part of a group (think of your favorite song collection) you probably recall those songs in a very specific order; your ABCs, or reciting a poem. Usually, the way this type of memory is stored is determined by just how much attention you gave to the learning process. As you can probably gather, few things actually have the honor of reaching your retrieval memory. To reach this point, the memory must be encoded deeply and have formed many connections over time.

Understanding these basic functions of how the memory works helps us to see why cramming for an exam is not an effective learning technique. When you spend long hours studying just before an exam, you are storing what you've learned in your short-term memory because you know it must remain there for at least a day or more. However, your level of attention begins to wane after a time because you don't really have a commitment to recall the information after you have completed the test. This means your motivation is not very strong so the brain will store the information in a space that exists somewhere between your long-term and your short-term memories. In other words, it won't be encoded deeply into your long-term memory and without reinforcement, it will begin to fade.

To accelerate your learning, you goal is to improve your memory capacity and train your brain to create deeper connections that will lock in your new knowledge for longer periods of time.

Forgetfulness

We all forget things from time to time. It is part of the human process However, when you are trying to improve your ability to learn you also need to focus on how to strengthen your memory so you don't lose what you are working so hard to learn. To do this, we really need to take a little time to figure out exactly why we forget things.

In truth, forgetfulness is simply a weakness in the brain's ability to store or to retrieve information. For example, if information is misfiled in the short-term memory banks rather than the long-term chances are if you need to recall it six-months later, it won't be available for retrieval. Your inability to find it is actually a problem with how deeply the information has been embedded.

There are three ways the brain will try to retrieve the information stored within it.

1. Recall
2. Recognition
3. Relearning

When you recall something you are remembering it without any prompting or cue. We do this when we recite lists of things without any external aids. We recall our ABCs, our home address, phone numbers, and our birthdays. These are so strongly embedded into our minds that we have no fear of forgetting them no matter what may happen. Most people can remember their first home address even though they have not lived there for decades. It's because it has been rehearsed repeatedly or you have placed a lot of importance to retaining this knowledge that the brain gives it considerably more attention than anything else.

Recall is the strongest form of memory you can have so it is also the most difficult to achieve. For something to be stored in your recall, you will usually have to dedicate many hours of practice or study to get it there yet, this is the area that we are targeting when we are trying to achieve accelerated learning.

Recognition is the type of memory that requires a cue to bring it to mind. We often do this type of memory when we hear one or two notes from a song. As soon as you hear those notes, your mind will immediately bring up the entire song in an instant but without that cue, it is almost impossible to remember. You also use recognition when you need to remember different associated facts. For example, you may not be able to remember all the countries of the world and their capitals but if you were given a clue, a rhyme or a song, it would be much easier for you to bring them to mind.

To use this to your advantage, try to create an unusual mental picture of your lesson so that your brain will latch onto it and you'll have a much better chance of recalling the information to mind when you need it. For this type of memory, mnemonics, and other similar study tools tend to work best. Since we may have a limited amount of time to dedicate to study, we naturally use these devices to group the new data together into recognizable chunks and rely on the cues to help us to remember them.

Finally, relearning - the weakest form of memory, occurs during the review process of study. It is a systematic approach where you use less and less effort to study it each time you access this type of information. For example, you may receive a specific list of information at work on Monday. The first day you receive the data, it may take you 30 minutes to get through it all but the next day, it may only require you to spend half that time. By the end of the week, you will probably get through it with a cursory glance.

However, if the data is only good for a single week, the following week you won't recall it because you haven't committed it to your long-term memory yet. This often happens when you learn a new language in school. You may be required to learn 20, 30 or more words every day and you will do well absorbing the information. By reviewing the information on a regular basis you may feel that you have mastered the topic. However, once class is over and you are no longer using that information, it will fade surprisingly quickly. This is where the expression "use it or lose it" comes from. When you store information in this stage, you have not yet taken the steps to put the information into your long-term memory banks so in time, no matter how good you may be at it, it will begin to fade.

So, it is easy to see that learning is not just about our ability to absorb new information but the key to its success is on enhancing our memory and making sure that what we absorb is encoded and stored properly for easy retrieval. Our brain's have a natural disposition to get rid of information as soon as it can, so we have to be ever diligent on how we store it from the very beginning.

We all have something called a "forgetting curve" where our brains slowly begin to sift out information after we have learned it. In essence, our memories begin to decay after a surprisingly short period of time if you do not take some action to reinforce it. For example, if you read a new lesson one day it may seem to have made a very strong impression on your mind, however, within just a few days, you're probably wondering what you really took in or if you've learned anything at all. Chances are, you will probably remember only half of it after as little as four days and in about a week, your memory will drop to around 30%.

The point here is that without review, in time, what you have learned will disappear to practically nothing. However, with regular review and practice, you can easily push your memory back closer to the 100% mark with just a little investment in time.

From just understanding how the brain sifts through information, discarding things that it does not perceive as valuable, it can help you to maximize the benefits you might receive from your study sessions. As you begin to learn about your forgetting curve, your goal with each study period is to reduce its decline, attempting to lower your percentages as much as possible by reducing the amount of memory decay you can naturally expect after each learning session.

To do this, we need to understand this type of decline better. According to some research studies, the rate of decline could be reduced if several factors are in place. First, this rate could significantly be reduced if the memory being stored was proven to have some level of personal significance and second, the age of the memory played a major role in how quickly we began to remember.

This informs us that there is little we can do to reduce the impact of information loss due to the forgetting curve, but it does suggest that there are things we can do to ensure that the information is stored in the proper area of our brains to make sure that it is easier to bring to mind when it is needed.

Our ability to remember information is our primary goal but we should expect more. As we have begun to realize, we should be continuously aiming for what we learn to reach recall memory above all else and recognition as our fallback goal. So, the question should now be, how to use this information to make us better and more efficient learners. The answer is simple, *retrieval practice.*

In the traditional sense, we consider learning to be a method where we absorb new information in our brains. A purely passive act, there is little of what we do invested into the learning process. However, now that we understand how memory works, we can see why this is only half of the learning process. When we learn something passively, we may come to understand it at the time but unless we personally invest in the study process, making study more of an activity, we are not likely to be able to retrieve that information later on when we need it.

This is where retrieval practice can be of help. Rather than getting into a continuous practice of accumulating more knowledge, we can stop periodically and pull information out of our brains instead. By making practical application of the knowledge we have already absorbed, we reinforce the memories we've already stored making them much easier to recall over time.

We can do this by using prompts to help us to put the memory to good use. One of the most common and familiar methods of retrieval practice is the use of flash cards. The front of the card is the cue and the back of the card is the information we've already learned. This is one of the best ways to boost your memory, especially when dealing with facts. Once you understand how it works, you'll see why this simple method of memory training is so effective.

First off, retrieval practice is an active skill. In your brain, it demands that you process the image or clue through thinking and searching out the data until you finally are able to retrieve the information you need. Repeated practice in this way will eventually move the memory from the recognition type of memory to recall where you will learn this information without the need of any clues to help you get to it.

How to Make Good Use of Retrieval Practice

One of the main reasons why retrieval practice has proven to be so effective is because it requires you to take an active role in the learning process. Rather than simply trying to absorb information that others give you, it is necessary for you to invest in actually doing something to reinforce the learning.

Now that we understand how our memories are stored and activated, we realize that retrieval practice is simply a means of making it easier for you to remember new things and "retrieve" these new concepts from the stores in our brain. So, in essence, learning should be more than just putting information in, it should also involve strategies that help you to pull it out when needed.

While flashcards are an excellent example of retrieval practice, we do not have to limit ourselves with these. In fact, they are not the actual strategy but merely a tool that allows us to apply the strategy in one form of retrieval practice. Actually, most people do not use flashcards to their best advantage and so do not really reinforce their learning in the right way.

For example, many use flashcards with a more passive approach. They see the cue, answer the card, flip it over to check their answer and move on to the next card. This may appear to be the obvious use but if if you change just one single element you can boost your memory even more. Simply by taking the added step of saying the answer **out loud** suddenly turns this into a more active form of study. This may seem like a pretty small difference but an essential one just the same. The act of vocalizing the answer before moving on actually engages more of your senses and involves more brain activity for the information to process.

Of course, in real life, there may not be any flashcards to rely on, there may not be a teacher around to give you the needed cues, and you may not have any additional external assistance to help you to retrieve the information you need. However, that does not mean that retrieval practice is not possible. We can still use flashcards as an example only using the basic methodology in more complex strategies.

Whether you're studying information for school or for work, you can create your own flashcards but instead of placing verbal cues or equations on the cards, try using concepts on the front and explanations on the back. Remember, earlier in the book we talked about learning concepts before facts. So, once you understand the concepts create flashcards for them following these basic rules:

- Reword the concepts in simple English
- Write a plot or an example that demonstrates the concept
- Apply the concept to a real-life experience
- Write the opposite of the concept
- Draw a visual image of the concept

So, rather than your flashcards written literally, you can write them so that they cover more abstract matters of the lesson. By using this approach, you actually push your brain to think beyond the written word and be able to extract more detailed information that may not actually be included in the lesson itself.

Once you've mastered those, then you can create another set of flashcards that deal with the minute details surrounding your particular concept. Placing all of the flashcards within the context of a concept will help you to gain a deeper understanding of them and find more immediate applications in real life.

Chapter 6: What Mistakes Really Mean

Learning can be either passive or active depending on how much you are willing to invest in it. You could think of it as if you are looking at the past and extracting concepts that may at first seem insignificant to you and sifting through them, searching out what they could really mean to your life and storing in a safe place until needed. There is no end to the different types of learning techniques you can use to help you to do this so it is very tempting to try all sorts of new and exciting ideas as you hear from them.

Unfortunately, many of those learning strategies could prove to be very ineffective and time consuming when you're trying to absorb that information at an accelerated rate. You can avoid this by learning how to identify these time wasters before you begin and creating your own methods for correcting them. This will help you to avoid making unnecessary mistakes that could lead to slowing down your learning process.

Have the Right Mindset

Again, it is important to consider your personal attitude towards learning. According to Dr. Carol Dweck of Stanford University, most people have either one of two primary mindsets in their approach to study.

Those with a **fixed** mindset hold to the belief that certain traits as intelligence and talent are inborn and genetic. Therefore, these things are something you either have or you don't and there is very little that can be done to change that. Those with this mindset usually do not do well in studies because they feel that their efforts will not yield results unless they are part of the select few that are born with the needed qualities to master the skills they are trying to achieve.

These are the people that will limit their studies so they only concentrate on areas where they are confident that they will succeed and take steps to avoid anything that may require them to struggle or create a possibility that they will fail. This allows them to avoid criticism, or to have to show any sign of weakness or flaws in their body of knowledge.

Those with a **growth** mindset however, are more willing to take on more challenging work. They feel that they can master any topic that holds their interest if they have enough tenacity and put in enough effort to do so. They are persistent enough to push through barriers, possible limitations, and aren't afraid of critical feedback from others but will use that information as inspiration to spur them onto more learning opportunities.

Your viewpoint in this regard will determine how you will view the challenges and setbacks that you receive. If you have a fixed mindset then likely you will conclude that your ability to learn that particular subject or skill is not within you reach. So, when you make a mistake, you will subconsciously view it as fate and there is little you can do about it. If on the other hand, you have a growth mindset, then you may view those same mistakes as a means to expand your skills, use them as stepping stones to your ultimate goal. It is clear from just this single point what type of view works best with the accreted learning method.

The results of several research studies emphasized this very point. Of the subjects studied, those with a fixed mindset focused more on the type of results that gave them a better chance at success while those with a growth mindset looked for opportunities that would allow them to expand their abilities. In essence, their view of success was different. One group saw learning something new as success while the other group viewed success as avoiding mistakes.

In addition, those with the fixed mindset found they were only interested in getting data that showed their present abilities with no expectations of change in the future whereas those with a growth mindset showed zero interest in getting the right answer but were instead concerned with any information that would allow them to grow in their knowledge and develop new skills and talents. They saw no negative aspect to getting the wrong answer but were interested in any information that will allow them to advance their personal development.

In short, those with the growth mindset were focused on learning while those with the fixed mindset were more focused on avoiding mistakes.

This type of mental development occurs when we are very young and if not adjusted later on will remain with us throughout our entire lifetime. The good news is that even though we may have a fixed mindset, it is not a permanent viewpoint but can be changed. Just like any other mental habit, we can learn to mentally switch to a growth mindset, thus making it possible for us to make sure that we continue to expand our knowledge every time we set out to learn something new.

We can change our viewpoint simply by applying intervention techniques. With very small, sometimes minuscule adjustments we can gradually begin to change the way we view learning in general.

One way to do this is with praise. When you compliment someone who has made a mistake you open up their minds just a tiny bit to allow a more positive viewpoint to start to take shape. Of course, you don't want to compliment the mistake itself, but you can always find something positive to say to someone. For example, you might see a mistake but compliment them on their approach to the answer like: "I can really see that you struggled with this problem but I admire the fact that you didn't quit. You now turn their focus to the process of learning the correct method without blatantly criticizing the specific mistake.

When you praise someone based on their skills or abilities, you are reinforcing the idea that the skill needed is not an inborn trait that cannot be changed. This is sort of like complimenting someone based on their genetic physical appearance. You are giving them credit for something they had no control over. However, praise the effort; how she did her hair, applied make up, or the selection of clothes, you are now looking at the effort they have put into enhancing their appearance. The action they they have taken. The goal is to compliment the effort not the genetics.

The more you praise the effort, the easier it will be for the person to be motivated to put in more effort in the future. This can be a practice you apply in everyday life, in all your interactions with other people. By making this a practice, you make it easier for others to accept constructive criticism, and build up the anticipation of learning new things in the future. By extension, by your practicing this type of praise and freely offering it to others, you also reinforce those same ideas into your own mind. You'll learn just how to evaluate your own behavior when you are faced with learning something completely new.

Another Way to View Mistakes

Often mistakes are not a result of a lack of effort on the part of the student. They could be a direct result of how the information was received during the lesson. We've already discussed how our minds are geared towards certain learning styles. Once we know what our primary form of intelligence is, it is easy to expect that if information is taught in that vein it will be much easier for us to absorb. However, we may not always have the luxury of receiving information in our preferred format. This does not mean that we can't learn but it may indicate that we will have to work a little harder to absorb the new information and in the process, we will make mistakes.

There are actually some biological factors that give support to this theory. Our multiple intelligences are not purely by accident. The structures of our brains are what actually make us strong in one area or another. Consider these biological facts:

Visual: Occipital lobes control the visual sense. The occipital and parietal lobes are key in controlling spatial orientation.

Aural: The temporal lobes are responsible for all your auditory content and the right temporal lobe is primarily used for music.

Verbal: Controlled by the temporal and frontal lobes primarily located in the Broca's and Wernicke's regions of the brain.

Physical: The cerebellum and the motor cortex located at the very back of the frontal lobe controls the majority of our physical movement.

Logical: Controlled primarily by the parietal lobe on the left side of the brain. The area that focuses on our ability to think logically.

Social: The frontal and temporal lobes are responsible for how we manage social activities. Our limbic system also has an influence on what we do in a social environment as well as what we do when we are alone. It controls our emotions and our moods.

Intrapersonal: Controlled mostly by the frontal and parietal lobes and our limbic system.

Even with these scientific facts before us, there is nothing to say that our brains are so fixed that we can't learn in different ways. For example, if a person were to lose his sights in an accident, losing his visual intelligence will not stop him from learning. He will however, need to build up his abilities in the other senses and eventually will be able to continue to learn. This is evidence that shows that even though we have a preferred form of intelligence, we have within us to ability to adapt and use other intelligences when needed.

The idea of multiple intelligences has met with a certain level of resistance due to the fact that some have concluded that you can't learn unless you acquire information in your preferred learning style. However, while it may be your preferred learning style, it is not your only learning style. In reality, you can learn in different styles as long as you are willing to adjust your level of focus and commitment to the study.

By concluding that you can only learn with one predominant style you are limiting yourself, which can only work to your disadvantage. It is true that based on these natural intelligences, you may gravitate more towards one style than another however, by reinforcing your learning through use of several different styles of learning you not only increase your chances of building up knowledge but you engage more of your brain activity in the entire process.

Remember, learning happens much faster when you are an active participant. You learn even better when you are motivated. So, find ways to become more active in the process from start to finish. This could mean taking notes, making it more meaningful to you, explaining it to others, etc. All of this could lead to errors in your conclusions however, you can choose to view those errors as a blight on your abilities or you can use them as stepping stones to better understanding.

Nearly all learning in life is based on the trial and error method. Making a mistake is not a reflection on your personal character or even on your ability to master a certain skill. You can choose to allow it to derail your learning process and discourage you or you can view that mistake as a way to practice new knowledge, a chance to find better solutions to the problem you already have and opening yourself up to grow in your knowledge.

Chapter 7: What Mistakes Really Mean

Once you have mastered your new knowledge or new skill, the learning process is not yet complete. If you are properly motivated, there is a good chance that you will want to do more than just learn this new topic, you'll also want to build on it and become expert in your field. To do this, it will become necessary for you to reinforce what you have already learned. There are numerous strategies that will help you to cement your new knowledge into your brain, some you will find will work well for you and others will not. Choose the ones that will work best for you or use the ideas generated here to create some methods that are more suited to your personal learning style.

10,000 Hours

While learning the basics of anything can be mastered in a few sessions, to become proficient in that same subject requires that you have to at some point stop learning and start doing. You can learn the fundamentals of anything from a book but if you ever hope to claim your experience in the skill or talent, you will at some point have to close that book and put what you've learned into practice.

Think about all the things that you learned in your life; riding a bicycle, swimming, dancing, or even just mastering the ability to read. While you may have understood the principles behind what you read, a time came when it was necessary to reinforce that knowledge with actual practice.

According to a research project designated to studying proficient violin players in Berlin, of those players that were most proficient, they averaged approximately 10,000 hours of practice over the course of building up their talent. Those that ranked on the average level only reported approximately 4,000 hours each.

This information helps us to see that in order to become "expert" in skill at any endeavor we might want to undertake, we need to stop studying and start practicing. Over the years, we have seen firsthand the benefits of extensive practice. While we may view these people as overnight successes, before these people were viewed as "experts" in their field by others, they had amassed countless hours of diligent practice and work to reach that point.

This type of rule can apply to just about anything we decide we want to learn. Few people take on a study project only to get a basic understanding of it but in fact, want to reach a point where they can excel in the subject. You can apply this to anything from cooking to zoology, the more time you set aside to practice what you have learned the stronger you entrench those teachings into your mind.

Learning is one thing, mastery is something else entirely. In order to become proficient in anything, you must be willing to invest both time and patience in your subject. This book is about accelerated learning not about becoming efficient in any prospect. So, as you begin to learn about different things, you will have to tailor your expectations so that you don't expect too much too fast. If you apply the techniques found in this book, you will learn at a faster pace but to develop an expert status, there is only one way to get there, with a regular commitment of time and realistic expectations.

Still, practice has to be done in a very specific way. If you are just working on something by rote, then your mind is not fully committed to it. Repetitious exercises will help you to develop muscle memory but will only allow you to establish a system of consistent movements throughout, making the more automatic. This type of practice does nothing to boost your level of intelligence.

Deliberate practice though, requires you to put more mental effort into the task, breaking it down into smaller and smaller parts, repeating them over and over again, taking mental note of the areas where you need to focus more attention on improvement. Deliberate practice is far more involved than just practicing by rote. While it involves mastering the things you understand, it also involves finding those weak areas and taking the initiative to find the information to fill in the gaps, rounding out your knowledge so that it is a complete package. It involves several steps.

- Identifying your needs
- Examining your weaknesses
- Finding possible solutions
- Testing your theories
- Getting feedback
- Refocusing your efforts

Continuing with these steps until you reach your overall goal helps you to practice in a way that will allow you to build your expertise and thus reinforce your knowledge in a way that you can grow from.

You must be careful though. There is the risk of slipping into mundane rote work if you can't keep your mind focused properly. You also need to give extra attention that you are in fact, reinforcing your knowledge in the wrong way. If you've learned the information correctly then everything will work well but if you didn't acquire the information correctly, you could end up simply reinforcing bad habits and not improving at all. This is why, it is often a good idea to get external feedback from experts to make sure you're on the right track.

Your goal should be not just to learn new knowledge but to learn it in such a way that you can apply it accurately. That way you will be able to identify the mistakes and find new ways to solve them correctly.

However, the results of newer research also tells us that in order to reinforce what we have learned, we need to do more than just practice it. Intensive practice has proved beneficial in certain areas like sports, music, games, and the arts but other areas weren't able to show such a significant increase, indicating that some professional goals you may have for yourself may need more than just practice to make sure that you find success.

The 80/20 Rule

The 80/20 rule is a common rule that simply states that within any given set of circumstances; only 20% of the components are considered to be important while the other 80% are trivial. This is an important reminder that everything we absorb through the learning process is not essential information that will help us to grow.

We see this in normal brain biology. Our brains are natural filters that sift out much of the data our senses collect every day. It carefully selects what information is important and should be remembered while your glimpse of the hummingbird you saw six months ago while you were watering your garden is not essential to what you need stored in your long-term memory.

As you study, it is important that you learn how to identify what that 20% of important information is. This can be applied in just about every avenue of life. Notice these facts:

- 80% of sales comes from 20% of customers
- 80% of company tasks are performed by 20% of the employees
- 80% of happy people are found in only 20% of relationships
- 80% of travels can be highlighted in only 20% of the experiences

These points only serve to reinforce the fact that all knowledge contains the ability to help you grow. You become expert in any area by making sure you're not wasting a lot of time on trivial points but can determine what points of the lesson are the most important.

This does not mean that you need to ignore everything else but the additional information should be considered as supplementary and does not need to take up the lion's share of your attention during the study time. Attack the important elements first and then once those are mastered, go back and address the supplemental information later.

Teaching Others

Probably, the most rewarding method for reinforcing your newfound knowledge is teaching it to someone else. When you are required to take your subject and break it down and explain it to others it not only cements the knowledge in your own mind but it also helps you to better identify the flaws in your own thinking.

By teaching others, you are able to see both sides of the learning process, which can give you valuable insight into how others absorb the same information. Their questions can prove to be very insightful in highlighting areas of the topic you may not have considered. It is probably the most active of all learning styles. Remember that the more engaged you are in the process the better you'll be able to master it. Consider these estimates:

- You remember 90% of what you learn if you teach others or use your new knowledge immediately
- You remember 75% when you practice what you learn
- You remember 50% when you participate in group discussions
- 30% when you observe a demonstration
- 20% if you watch an audio-visual presentation
- 10% if you read it
- 5% if you listen only

These are mere estimates of what retention is but it does go to show that the more involved you are in the process the better your ability to learn.

There is no question that teaching is about as active as it can get. It not only cements the information in your mind but it forces you to look at the matter from different angles, exposing gaps in your understanding and sending you back to the basics to find the answers you need. It's a way of testing your knowledge and proving to yourself if you know it or not.

Chapter 8: Preparing to Learn for Life

Learning is a lifelong experience that doesn't stop when you finish school. Our brains have been uniquely designed so that it is in constant search of new information so we all need to rethink the common viewpoint that says that we should stop learning at a certain point. In fact, a significant part of life's experiences stem from our learning. We marvel at the wonders of the universe, technology is constantly advancing, and knowledge in today's modern age is growing exponentially year after year. We need to be consistent learners just to keep up with the constant changes in our every day life. In order to be successful in this type of endeavor, we need to view learning as a life habit rather than just a phase we go through.

Habits are activities we do so much that they become a part of our subconscious behavior. We do these things automatically, without thought, in much the same way as we might view chewing our food when we eat. Becoming an accelerated learner may not be easy at first. We may have to practice these techniques repeatedly until we reach a point where we can slip into learning mode and are able to make it a natural part of our lives.

When learning becomes a habit, it's a clear indication that we have mastered the skill so well that we don't need to give it extra thought. It then becomes part of our recall memory. But how do you develop your learning skills to that point? There are several things you must keep in mind.

Be Persistent

Your ability to remain focused on your lessons and follow through even when things are tough will help you to develop good learning habits. When you consistently work to create new strategies to tackle those big problems and refuse to let them discourage you, eventually, you'll reach a point where learning will become second nature to you. However, in order to accomplish this, you will have to become comfortable with dealing with things that may not be very clear, to be okay when things are not laid out plainly in black and white. You'll also need to develop some flexibility in your study plan. Give yourself some options so you're not falling into a rut of repeating the same things over and over again. This way, you'll be more likely to have an open mind when tackling new problems and challenges as they present themselves.

Another element of persistence is patience. This may not be a problem when the learning is easy and information is readily understood, but frustration tends to step in when you are faced with problems that are difficult to understand. It's coming to grips with the idea that you will meet with obstacles that may restrict your comprehension, that you will make mistakes, and you will face challenges. If you are persistent, you won't allow these factors to disrupt your learning but will use them skillfully in forging ahead until you reach the point of mastery.

It will require a certain level of self-discipline so you can remain focused and approach your learning in a deliberate manner. The impulse may be to throw it all aside for something easy, but resisting that urge and pushing through will be the key to your success. Learning to think before giving into impulse reactions will help you to accomplish what you set out to do and will keep you on the path to accelerated learning.

Be Flexible

A good learner will be flexible enough to adapt their techniques to the problems before them. Mental flexibility will allow you to develop an open mind so that you can shift your thinking when you reach a point where you face an obstacle. Rather than allowing that to block your growth, if you are flexible enough, you will find ways around the problem and approach it from a completely different angle if need be.

Flexibility also means overcoming preconceived ideas about what you believe to be true. This is much easier to do if you enter the learning process with positive emotions rather than allowing negative feelings to come into play. Remember, you're looking for a long-term solution to a problem and not some type of quick fix. While you may have previously believed that the solution to a problem is one way, leave yourself open to alternatives that you may uncover during your studies that could make the process easier.

Reach for Quality, not Quantity

When you are studying with the aim of being accurate, your time will produce quality results. It's not how much you study it is how much you get from your study. When your focus is on acquiring the right information rather than how much information, you are less likely to make mistakes in your hurry to the finish line; you'll pay more attention to detail, check, and then double check your results so you can be sure that the finished product of your efforts will yield reliable results that you can use going forward.

Because of this, you'll be less likely to take shortcuts but take your study seriously. While you can ask others for help, try to only get them to give you options and don't rely on them to do the heavy lifting for you. This is your learning experience and the more you trust yourself to work out the problems the more benefit you will receive from it.

To become a lifelong learner, means that you will have to not just approach a learning session as a one-time event but see every lesson you undertake as a major part of your life. Learning should not be viewed as something you do in addition to your normal routine but it should be a part of who you are as a person. Learn to love to learn and when you do, you will be able to develop the kind of habits that will provide you with all you need to continue to grow in knowledge and wisdom until the very end of your days.

Conclusion

Thank you again for downloading this book!

I hope this book was able to help you to be able to develop those skills that will help you to benefit from being a lifelong learner.

In this book we have discussed a lot of information that will not only make you a better student but will help you to develop the habits that have earmarked people for success for generations. We have learned:

- How your mental state of mind can impact how you learn

- How your brain receives and processes information

- How to M.A.S.T.E.R learning by following the six-step plan to accelerate your learning

- How to prepare your mind so it is more receptive to learning

- How to boost your memory so that you can access your wealth of new knowledge

- And how to reinforce all that new knowledge so that it is less likely to fade over time

Learning is not something that we do simply as a means to get by. In today's modern age, knowledge is growing at an impressively rapid rate making it necessary for all of us, young and old, to be on a continuous learning cycle. Never before in our human history has so much information been so easily accessible, and it is changing constantly.

This means that we have to be ever vigilant in keeping our minds open to new shifts in how our world works. The only way to successfully navigate such rapid moving waters is to accelerate your learning so that you can grow right along with the rest of the world. By applying these simple basic strategies contained here in this book, you will not only be able to keep up with the rapid flow of information coming your way, you'll be able to enjoy it to.

The next step is to take this information to heart and put it into practice.

Finally, if you enjoyed this book, then I'd like to ask you for a favor, would you be kind enough to leave a review for this book on Amazon? It'd be greatly appreciated!

Thank you and good luck!

Accelerated Learning

How to learn like Einstein - Read faster, memorize more and master anything with ease

Including DIY-exercises!

Patrick Lightman

Introduction

In my school days, things were taught one way and one way only. This wasn't good for a student like me. Like most people, I caught on to some subjects quickly and excelled at them. Other subjects, I didn't understand speedily and not only lost interest in them but made poor grades in those subjects as well.

Somehow, in the lower grades, I managed to pass just by the skin of my teeth to the next grade level. Junior High and High School weren't as forgiving as the lower grades.

I got one chance to pass a class and more than once I failed the subject and had to repeat it. I thought of this as an embarrassment, but each class proved to be a blessing.

Algebra and Biology were my hardest classes. The first teachers I had for these classes were strict and flatly refused to give me extra attention to help me pass their classes. I had to sink or swim, and I drowned.

The next year, I had to retake the classes, and you can bet your sweet tushy that I signed up for different teachers for those classes. And what a genius idea that was.

After all, I didn't learn a darn thing from the other teachers, why not give someone else a try? So that's what I did. Coaches who also taught my hardest classes became my new teachers. With their help and new ideas on how to help kids learn things easier, I excelled at my worst subjects for the first time since I'd started school. I even received awards for making straight A's in both classes, under the coaches' careful guidance.

What did they do that the other teachers didn't?

They took the time to get to know each student, talk to them a bit, understand them. Both of my coach slash teachers came to find that I could memorize anything if they gave me small amounts at a time.

I couldn't memorize fifty biology definitions in one hour – the time allotted for each class. What I could do was memorize five of them in one hour. When the final test came, and I'd remembered fifty definitions, but at a speed of five a day, I aced those tests.

In Algebra, the same situation was found. I couldn't do twenty problems in one hour. I could do five to seven problems each classroom hour. And the thing was that without the added pressure of making sure I got all twenty problems done in an hour's time, I was able to calm down and focus on the small tasks at hand. The freaking out and berating myself for being stupid were over. I was achieving the goals set for me, and I was doing it with ease.

Those coaches knew what they were doing back then. Thankfully, those men were at the forefront of what would become a new way of teaching and learning. That meant that more people could achieve what they wouldn't have been able to in the not so distant past.

In this book, I'm going to give you some great ideas on how to spark your learning energy. If one way doesn't work for you, try another, and another until you find what does work for you. Something will work for you; I virtually promise that.

Give yourself time to practice each style. If after a while that's just not working for you, try something else. One of my sons continuously flunked his spelling tests when he was in second grade. The teacher had him doing the usual thing, writing the spelling words five or even ten times each. That wasn't working for him.

One day, not knowing what the heck else to do for him, I told him to stare at the list of words for about a minute right before he had to take the spelling test. And that boy got a perfect score on that test and all the rest of the spelling tests he took from then on. So there is more proof that there are more ways than one to learn anything.

It's a wonderful time to be a student. So get ready to not only read about how to accelerate your learning but enjoy doing it too!

Chapter 1

Shattering Old Paradigms

'Any fool can know. The point is to understand.' –Albert Einstein

Paradigms are patterns. In learning, there have been established models to teach children. In the subject of spelling, it has been the rule to write spelling words multiple times.

As a writer who spells words every day, I can tell you that this doesn't always work. For some reason, I always misspell certain words. Conscious and conscience are the worst for me and don't get me started on any of the words with 'ph's in them that are spoken as an 'f' - what a horrible trick to play on innocent children!

In the traditional way of teaching subjects, textbooks are the main point of the entire class. Now, some textbooks are interesting. But far more of them are downright boring. I'm sure you've had your fair share of textbooks that lulled you to sleep on a sunny afternoon of doing homework at the kitchen table.

For such a long time, using textbooks has been the teacher's only form of teaching students. The sad part of that is, not everyone can learn that way. Simply reading something doesn't mean you've mastered it especially when the text is uninspiring.

Watching films about history on television is incredible. Reading about historical events in a textbook is – well, tiresome to say the least. Kids nowadays need inspiration to learn. And boy, can they learn when inspired!

There are still adults to this day who have no clue how to hook up video game systems. But you can bet your bottom dollar that their five-year-old is a wiz at the task. And that kid didn't have to read one single set of instructions to do it either.

How does this happen?

Learning by watching is how this happens. That kid watched an older kid hook up the gaming system many times before they took on the task. The parent stands back; sure the child won't succeed at what they'd failed at. When the television comes on, and the system is up and running, you can bet the parent has a dropped jaw and a look of utter confusion on their faces.

In the old way of learning, it's the teacher's job to make sure each student knows the material word-for-word. The questions on the tests wanted specific answers that came from the textbook. Answers in your own words would've been counted as wrong. If the text read, Sam Hill was at the Battle of Hastings on the sixth of July, fifteen, fifty-seven, then that's what the answer had better be.

Many a time I had disagreements with my teachers as to why I wrote my own words, instead of those written in the oh-so-right textbooks. And the thing is, that now, with a plethora of informative facts and information at our fingertips, we've learned that some of that information in textbooks is wrong. That's right!

That's why forward-thinking teachers invite their students to research things in every subject. If Tommy thinks the information the teacher is giving the class is wrong, he can do his research to prove his point. More likely than not, he'll find the teacher is right. But now that he's seen that to be true on his own, it's cemented in his mind a lot more securely than if he'd been told to take her word for it.

In the old way of learning, teachers taught, the class stayed quiet and listened to her lecture or read. This didn't require interaction between class members or the class with the teacher. You sat still, kept your mouth shut, and tried desperately not to fall asleep.

In the new way of teaching, the teacher encourages the class to give their opinions, their ideas, their valuable input. Everyone wants to feel that they are valued, and in school, it's no different. With today's exciting advances in learning, each child can participate without fear of getting something wrong.

It was Walt Disney who said, 'Our greatest natural resource is the minds of children.' I believe that to be truer today than ever. If children are viewed as essential parts of the classroom, then the learning can be done by all the members of that classroom, even the teacher.

The shift in the learning paradigm isn't something to be afraid of. This shift means that more people than ever in history will have vast amounts of knowledge about many things.

If you have trouble reading – say you've got dyslexia – then you can learn in other ways. If you can't hear well, but you can read and retain everything – then you can still learn without needing to listen to a teacher giving a lecture. There's more than one way to skin a cat – an unpleasant euphemism, but entirely accurate. If you can't learn one way, there are more ways to get that knowledge into your blossoming brain. It's all up to you to make it happen.

Gone are the days when you learned about skeletal systems by looking at one dimensional drawings inside of a textbook. With today's technology, you can use a 3D printer to see the skeletal systems as if you were looking at the real thing. You can get your hands on the skeleton as you learn the names of each bone.

Pointing at a drawing on a page, versus holding the bone in your hand makes a world of difference to your brain. Imagine watching each bone being formed in the process of 3D printing, and calling out the bone in progress. Everyone is interacting. Everyone is having fun. Everyone is learning.

Now, picture the same subject taught in another classroom, several years back. Students sit at their desks, keeping quiet. A teacher stands in front of them, the textbook in her hand, showing the class the picture in the book. She points out the different bones, asks you to look at the page and put your finger on the same bone she is. Have you learned much from that?

Most likely not. But the other way, the hands-on way – well, you probably felt excited to see the 3D process and to get actually to hold the bones that were made. And then – after all the bones are made – you get to put them together and make the skeleton. Now that's an activity you won't soon forget.

If things just stayed the same way, then we wouldn't have the burst of information available to us that we now have. The internet is like this living river of ever-evolving information. That includes knowledge of how people around the whole world learn effectively. We can use what others have learned. We can come up with ideas of our own to help others learn things that come hard to them.

To help you gain a leg up on others, to allow you to accelerate your learning, I'm going to share with you what I've researched. Gone are the days of textbooks and lectures. Gone are the days of sitting in silence in a classroom while a teacher drones on and on. Gone are the days where you sit still and read words that flow together without making a bit of sense to you and end up putting you to sleep.

We've got new ways of learning – stimulating ways – exciting ways. What skills will you need to achieve success? What plans do you need to make to start learning faster and retaining the information you've learned? How can you get yourself in the appropriate state of mind to begin learning in an accelerated fashion?

If you want to begin the process of learning at a higher speed, then you've got to build the right set of skills to do that. Learning how to get our head in the game when game time begins is essential. One cannot be distracted when one is trying to learn things quickly. If you don't have the proper plan, you won't succeed. If you follow this plan, you will have a much higher chance of succeeding.

Failure happens to the best of us. I don't want you to be disappointed by failing. What I want is for you to see that the route you took wasn't the route for you and take another one – for there are many.

If you want to learn faster, what is the one thing you need to learn how to do first?

Reading at an accelerated pace is key to learning more quickly. Taking the right kinds of notes is critical too. Why waste time on things that don't matter to your subject?

What about learning how to memorize in a way you've never dreamt possible? Wouldn't that make learning more natural and more efficient for you?

At times, we all have to cram for something. Would you like to learn the proper way to do that so you can ace the tests that you didn't have tons of time to study for?

How would you like to show what you know to others? Not only will it help them, but it will also make you feel like an effective teacher and leader who likes to help others achieve their goals.

You will learn all of this and even more by reading this action-packed book that will change the way you learn. And along the way, you can practice what you've learned by doing some of the, 'Do It Yourself or DIY exercises' at the end of each chapter.

Just like this one:

The paradigm shift benefits who?

(a)   Your grandparents?

(b)   Teachers?

(c)   You?

(d)   or both b and c?

On a scale of 1 to 10, how excited are you to learn how to accelerate your learning?

I hope you said 10 because this is something to be excited about. You're about to have a lot more time on your hands to do other things, rather than studying your hind end off for mediocre or even bad grades.

So, let's get started!

Chapter 2

The Keys to Effective Learning

'A man who reads too much and uses his own brain too little falls into lazy habits of thinking.' –Albert Einstein

Libraries of the past were full of books and little else. Nowadays one can go to their school or local library and get on a computer if they'd like. Before the age of computers, you'd be going to look through an index file for the card with the Dewey Decimal System number of the book you wanted to read or find research in. This number let the reader know where to find the book on the shelves of the library. A tedious chore, thankfully that is no more.

With the ease of gathering information from computers, learning has never been easier. So let's delve into some vital properties in the learning process. Once you've got these on your radar, everything else is a piece of cake.

Probing abilities proves useful when the person who is learning looks into the subject at hand. Hungering for information is key when learning something new. Get ready with your questions about the subject or task at hand. Don't be afraid to ask your questions, but be sure to listen if others ask the same or a similar question to yours, so the teacher doesn't become aggravated that you aren't listening to others in your group or class.

Once your questions are answered, move forward with the newfound knowledge to test the conclusions you and others come up with. In order to do that, be sure to accurately determine the problems and the plans of action before you get to your conclusions.

When solving problems both in life and in your classes, you should face each problem with a plan of action. You've got a messy bedroom – your parents say you can't play until you've got it cleaned up – what do you do?

You look at the problem, make a plan on how to best get it done, the fastest way possible, and you get to it, right?

Well, if you're smart, you do it that way. You start by identifying what needs to be done first, second, third, and so on so you can get outside to play with the other kids.

It's the same with any problem you find in your classes as well. Find the shortest route to get the problem dealt with and out of your way so you can move on to other things.

Have you ever heard of creative thinking?

You've probably been asked to think outside of the box on occasion. This means they want you to use your creative skills to solve a problem. The standard way could be used, but you're asked to come up with an alternative way to do something.

Imagination comes into play now. Don't be bashful about what you come up with, be brave and see what happens. Sure, some people might laugh, but that's okay. Not everyone understands what your unique imagination comes up with. In the end, all that matters is that the problem gets solved.

Information processing and evaluation skills are essential too. Not only should you know where to gather information from, but you also need to know what the heck to do with it once you've got it.

Putting the information into an order that makes sense is essential. Evaluating what's most important and going down the line from there is key.

Being aware of yourself is another important thing you must do in the learning process. Know what kind of learner you are – such as a hands-on learner or a reading learning or a listening learner.

You should also know what kinds of feelings you tend to have strongly. If you experience anxiety, then you know it can get in the way of your learning process. Learn to control that so that you and others who are learning around you can concentrate on the task at hand.

And on the subject of having difficulties learning yourself, try your best to have empathy for the problems others have too. Put yourself in their shoes and try not to antagonize their setbacks, the same way you would want them to do for you.

Communicating in a way that makes it easy for others to understand what it is you want or are explaining is another key factor in the learning process. You can practice your communication skills all the time; at home, at school, on the school bus, and when you're out and about.

Think about when you're at a restaurant and ordering what you want to eat. You want the person taking your order to get it right, so you're careful what you say to them. You want them to understand you, so that you get what you want. Do that with everything, and you will see great results from that one small thing.

Along with excellent communication skills comes the ability to motivate people. A motivator is a natural leader. If you know how to do something that others don't know how to do or are having a tough time learning, then help them out. Speak up, let them know that you can help out.

The world needs people like you to help others who aren't as effective at communicating. This one skill will benefit you the most. Take what you learn and pass that knowledge on, so others can know it too. Be a productive part of your group or classroom. It will not only give you a sense of pride, but it will help others build their levels of pride in themselves too.

In short, what each person needs in order to be a successful learner is easy to remember. First, you must identify the problem. Next, you need to know where to look for the information you will need to deal with this problem. Once you've got that information, you may not have all the tools required to deal with your problem effectively. You might have to use some creative thinking to get the job done.

Once you've successfully solved your problem, you might want to help others solve their problems. You can do this in many ways. Communicating effectively, knowing what your shortcomings are and dealing with theirs with a sense of empathy and compassion are key.

Not being afraid to lead when others have no one to follow is another way you can help your fellow students and others in your community as well. Once you know how to solve a problem, don't be afraid to let others know what you've found out. Helping others isn't only a nice thing to do; it'll help build your self-esteem while assisting them to develop theirs.

Learning can be easy when we all help each other. Learning can be fun when we pull together to take on each part of a task in our unique ways. Understanding and support as well as letting yourself and others think outside of the box can make learning a thing you strive to continue to do for your entire life.

Here are some DIY exercises that you can do to practice what you've learned in this chapter.

Probing abilities question: When going from point A to point B which is three miles away and you have a group of twelve people who need to be moved at the same time, what kinds of options do you have to get them there?

Problem-solving question: Jerry has two quarters. Don has two dimes and a nickel. Roy has five nickels. A bag of chips costs one dollar. All three boys would like to have some chips for a snack. What should they do to fix this problem that all three of them have?

Creative thinking question: Joe gathers the chickens' eggs from the coop the same way each time. He fights the hens to get off their nests so he can take their eggs and put them in his basket. What's another way Joe can gather the eggs without upsetting the chickens?

Information gathering, processing, and evaluation question: When putting together a brand new bicycle that has come inside of a box and is nothing but parts, where would you find the information on how to put the object together?

Empathy question: Joe is trying to tie his shoelaces and is having trouble doing the task. He's mad and saying how stupid he is. What could you do to help him out, without tying his shoes for him?

Motivation question: Jane is having trouble with her math assignment. She's too shy to ask anyone for help, but you see her fidgeting in her seat, chewing on her fingernails, and not writing anything down at all. What can you do to help motivate Jane in a way that helps her get the problem done?

Great work!

Chapter 3

Setting Yourself Up For Success

'A person who never made a mistake never tried anything new.' - Albert Einstein

Are you ready to try something new that will help you accelerate your learning?

Great.

And don't let the fear of making mistakes get in your way. We all make them. Mistakes are an essential part of the learning process, accelerated or not. You won't always do the right thing the first time. The great thing is that at least you'll know the wrong way to do it and won't do it that way again.

Even when you follow a plan, you might find yourself making mistakes. That's okay; it's human even. What you need to do then, is not beat yourself up about it. Shrug your shoulders, erase what you had, then move on. Don't let getting it wrong a time or two, or even three or four get you down. Just keep on trying.

With a plan or a framework, you've got a set of things to keep you going. This is especially helpful to those people who find it hard to find where to start a task or assignment. Getting overwhelmed isn't the most productive way to start anything. Having a set of things to do helps you not to get overwhelmed in the first place.

Each step is important so don't go skipping steps or skipping around. They're in order for a very good reason. The order simplifies things for you so that you can get your assignments done not only more accurately, but faster too.

Accelerated learning is all about speed and accuracy. With each building block I give you, you will become faster. With each step of the processes you learn, you will gain accuracy. In the end, you will become a genius who can easily take over the world.

What?

Just kidding.

But you will have the tools you need to make things happen for you. Mastering these skills means you will master your learning process. Anyone knows that being the master of your own fate is the key to not only a happy existence, but it's also key to the success you have in life.

The skills you will learn in this book won't only help you in school; they will help you for your entire life if you continue to practice them. So if you're ready to start making some real strides where your ability to learn is, then let's talk about M.A.S.T.E.R. framework and what it means for you.

The letter, 'M' is for 'mindset.' What your mindset is when you're presented with a learning opportunity directly affects how you take in the knowledge given to you. For instance, if you're tired, grouchy, and downright ornery, when your teacher gives you a history assignment about Jesse James, then you might not be too happy about that.

You might type in his name in the Google search engine, see that he was a criminal in the old west and write a report based on just that information alone. Being surly, you'd probably use the minimum amount words possible to get the bare facts on the man. Paying attention to small details would seem like a thing that would only waste your precious time too. And you'd do that all because of what your mindset was.

If you'd slept great the night before, had waffles for breakfast – your favourite – and had the cute girl in your homeroom class smile at you on the way in, then you might be in a completely different mindset.

If your mindset was happy, energetic, and hopeful, then when you got the assignment you might've gone a few steps further. You would've looked up Jesse James, saw that he was an outlaw in the wild west and thought you'd died and gone to Heaven. What an opportunity to delve into the life of a man who lived on his terms. Whether you agreed with his lifestyle or not, you've got that mindset that has you feeling like you not only want to know everything there is to know about the man, you want others to know too.

Mindset is the difference between poor work and great work. So if you're mindset is off, your work will be too.

Once you've got your mind under control - a cookie and some milk always help me to be happy and ready to gain some knowledge – now you've got to acquire the knowledge. Acquire is the 'A' in M.A.S.T.E.R.

Not only do you have a plethora of knowledge within a computer and the internet, but you've also got great television shows too. If you're not that kind of learner, there are books in both paperback and ebook forms to help you acquire the knowledge you will need for the task you've been presented with. Pick a form and get going on it.

Next, we have the letter, 'S' which stands for 'Search out the meaning.' Not all problems you are faced with will be something you can easily find information on. You may have to use different keywords or look in areas you hadn't thought to look before. Information on every subject is available somewhere; you've just got to look very hard sometimes. Other times it's easy to find. But be ready to look hard and search for what you'll need to be able deal with your specific problem or goal

'T' stands for 'Trigger your memory.' What if you're presented with a problem that you've dealt with before? Or what if the problem you've been given has aspects of something you've dealt with before?

Don't hesitate to fall back on your memory. When trying to solve a problem, use everything you can, your own memory included.

Now that you've done all those things, you're ready to put the 'E' in M.A.S.T.E.R. 'Exhibit what you know.' This is where you put what you now know into writing, or drawing, or putting together a slideshow – whatever the assignment calls for, you're ready to put it together.

When exhibiting what you know, make it sharp. You want to impress not only your teacher, but others, and yourself as well. Take pride in what you know and let the exhibit show that pride.

The 'R' is for 'Reflect on your learning.' You've put a lot into your research. You've learned a lot by putting it all together. Take the time to sit back and think about what it is that you've learned. Don't let all that time that it took to figure out where to get the information for your task go to waste. Don't let the time it took to gather all the information and facts get lost in the shuffle. Take time to feel the pride for a job well done.

It wasn't easy. It wasn't quick. It took time, patience, and more than a little understanding to get the task done, sit back and think about all that went into it and all that came out of it.

If you do all these steps, then each assignment will get a little easier as you do more of them. What once took days, now can take hours. What once took hours, can now take minutes. With these tools to help guide you through the process, you will only get faster and faster. Along with that, you will get more and more accurate. Your grades will climb as an after-effect.

But grades aren't all that matter here. The knowledge you acquire with each assignment you are given is worth more than A's or B's. The knowledge you obtain from your studies – if gained correctly – will stay in your mind for a lifetime.

Once we learn something and learn it the right way, we have that embedded in our brain. Sometimes, especially as we get older, we might not even be able to recall were that kernel of knowledge came from, but it's still there.

Now let's do some exercises to see if we understand how to use the M.A.S.T.E.R. framework.

What is the first and most crucial step in beginning an assignment?

(a)   Eat breakfast.

(b)   Take a hot shower.

(c)   Get into an argument with your older brother who hogged the cereal.

(d)   Get your mind clear and ready to learn, make sure your mindset is good.

When presented with a problem or an assignment, what is the best way to answer the questions asked?

(a)   Ask a friend.

(b)   Stare at the teacher until she tells you the answers.

(c)   Acquire the knowledge yourself.

(d)   Throw a shoe at Tony across the room and hope some answers pop out of him.

Can your own memory of things help you solve a problem?

(a)   No way, you've got to look up the answers each and every time.

(b)   Sure, you can trust your memory as long as you're sure it's spot on.

(c)   Memory, what memory?

How can you get all that knowledge you've obtained out to the masses so they can know it too?

(a)   Tell a close friend and ask them not to tell anyone else.

(b)   Exhibit what you know by writing a stand out paper on the subject.

(c)   Just stay quiet; no one needs to know how smart you are.

Chapter 4

Analyze and Understand Yourself

'Few are those who see with their own eyes and feel with their own hearts.' – Albert Einstein

How much do you really know yourself? How honest are you about the type of person that you are? And how many people would agree with you about the way you think of yourself?

Briefly, I've touched on the subject of mindset when you are trying to accelerate your learning. Seeing just how important this step is, I've written an entire chapter on it to help you understand not only the importance of having the right mindset before attempting to learn something new, but also how to achieve this sometimes difficult task.

If you've ever been in a foul mood and had something you had to achieve, even the most mundane task, you know it can be hard to motivate yourself to do anything. Something as easy as washing the dishes can be put off by having a bad mood get in your way.

Sometimes it can be as easy as whistling away the mood to help you get your mind right. Other times nothing seems to work. If you are faced with learning something new, being in a bad mood won't help you accomplish anything.

How many ways are there to pull yourself out of a bad mood?

Plenty.

That's the good news. There are plenty of ways to get yourself out of the mood. Watch something funny. With the internet at all of our fingertips most of the time, it's easy to find something to make you laugh.

Laughter is the best medicine as they say. And it's completely true too. Laughter has been proven to take away the blues and even strengthen your immune system. It is a miracle cure for many things, including that bad mood that is stopping you from learning something new.

If you can't manage to find anything to make you laugh your way out of that bad mood, then try something else. Exercise is another thing that can help you get out of your own head enough to push something like that away. If you hate to do exercises, then simply take a walk. Smell the roses on the way too. Let your spirit rise with each step you take.

In no time you should be feeling better and more optimistic about the day, the time at hand, and the future.

But let's say it's not just a bad mood that has you in a funk and not in the right frame of mind to learn. Let's say that you did something foolish right before class. Let's say that you ate a heavy meal that's made you sleepy. You've got a new subject coming up that you really need to do well in. But you've went and messed up your ability to pay attention as your mind is now on nothing but sleeping off the heavy meal.

Well, once done, you can't take it back. So make sure not to overindulge in anything before you know you're going to have to really put your mind to something. Thinking ahead is key to making sure you are in a resourceful state of mind when it really matters.

Confidence is key as well. Those of us who don't always have an abundance of confidence sometimes have to build it up. How can we do something like that?

Well, first of all, give yourself credit where credit is due. Did you ace that test last week? Then give yourself a pat on the back for a job well done.

Did you wash your mother's car a few days before, just to be nice? Well, then there's another kudos for you. Another feather in your cap, as they say. You did something nice for no reason at all. Look at you, you darling, you.

So, you're a nice person who has achieved some great things in the past. And you know that you can do that again. You learned how to tie your own shoes, you learned how to brush your own teeth, you learned how to walk and talk at the same time. You're a genius!

You can do this. You can learn new things and you can achieve the goals you set for yourself.

What if you're all keyed up? What if you just can't sit still? What if your heart is pounding, your palms are sweeting, and you feel like you might pass out?

Telling yourself to chill probably won't work for you. If you've gotten yourself all worked up over something, the best thing to do is deal with that before trying to deal with anything else.

Maybe your dog ran away from home and you're upset about it. Maybe your mind is on where the dog could be. Maybe you want to be searching your neighbourhood, instead of learning the anatomy of a goat.

But learning the anatomy of a goat is what your task for class is that day. What do you do?

Here's what I do when I find myself in a tizzy. I take several deep breaths. I hunch my shoulders together, hold them that way for ten seconds, then release them. That act allows tension to leave your system. Now breathe, feel your body relaxing. Wiggle your fingers, your toes, let the tension leave your body through the ends of your phalanges – those are your fingers and toes. Just learned something new right there, didn't you?

The point is to get the air into your lungs, let the bad energy leave your body with each exhale you make. Don't put any pressure on yourself at all about anything.

Learning isn't supposed to make you tense. It's supposed to make you feel charged up.

I'm sure you've seen the cartoon of someone thinking and a light bulb goes off above their head. That's because in reality when you get an idea or understand something, that feeling actually occurs. You get a zap of good energy and it makes you want to move on and learn more.

 Relaxing your mind helps you to learn things easier and faster. You can think of this in a physical manner. You've got to get from point A to point B. The road is full of potholes that you must avoid or your car will break an axle on them. Along with that problem, there's a terrible storm and you can barely see a thing. Add to it, a screaming baby brother in the backseat who wants his bottle. How can you have a relaxed mind if all this is going on?

It might seem impossible, but it is entirely possible. I've done it on many occasions.

The key is to block all that other stuff out. You have a goal here. You need to get from one place to another and you would love it if you got there alive, and with the car in one piece.

The weather might be making it hard, but you have windshield wipers and you also have control of the speed of your car. You can make it through the storm if you use your head to step on the brakes when you need to and to accelerate when you can.

Those potholes aren't helping matters. But if you go slow enough, you can avoid them. Even if you must go through some of them, going slowly will get it done without breaking your car.

So, there's that pain in the butt baby brother crying his head off. You've been here before. Mom is calling you for supper, but you're in the middle of a video game. And not just any game either. This is for all the marbles. This one is going to mean you're the supreme ruler of the universe. So, what did you do?

You totally blocked her out is what you did. She probably had to come shake you out of your mindset to get you to hear her. So do that with the other undesirable noises as well. Not that your mother's voice is undesirable, but you get what I'm throwing at you.

So now that you're in a resourceful state of mine. You've got yourself relaxed too. You've got that confidence up and going full steam. Your mindset is on the task at hand too. But something just isn't there.

What is it?

Motivation.

We all need motivation now and then. How do we get it?

As a writer, I've sat ay my computer with my head on straight. A blank page before me. All the confidence in the world as I've written award winning novels. I'm not worried, upset, or even bothered by anything. But nothing is happening. My fingers hover over the keys, but nothing happens.

What can I do to motivate myself?

In this case, reading something in the genre I'm going to be writing in is what motivates me. In your case, reading what others have said about the task you're about to take on might motivate you.

I'm sure you can recall a time when you were sitting around, watching cartoons when you got a text from Joey down the street. He said he's got this new game and he's really excited about it. There are ninjas in it and wild rabbits. It's the bomb.

Suddenly, watching racoons chase little kids isn't so interesting anymore. No, you want to play that ninja rabbit game. You've become motivated. And there are many ways you can make this happen for you too. Just keep trying until you find what works for you.

Here are some exercises to help you learn how to get into the right mindset to accelerate your learning:

When you go out to work in the garden, what resources would you use to help you out?

(a)   A bowl, a spoon, and a frying pan.
(b)   A rake, a shovel, and some seeds.
(c)   Your mom, your dog, and the lady from next door who's always looking out her window at you.

When you need to relax you?

(a)   Jump up and down.
(b)   Get into a race car and head down a busy street
(c)   Try out some new Yoga poses and breathing techniques.

You have to write five questions for your next assignment that deal with Socialism, what do you do to get in the right mindset?

(a)   Go bowling.
(b)   Watch a documentary about a socialist country.
(c)   Ask your mother to cut your fingernails for you.

You've been asked to give a speech at your school about how to keep the bathroom stalls clean. How do you find the confidence to pull this off?

(a)   You go sit in the bathroom for hours to get ready.

(b)   You ask the lunch lady to write you a speech.

(c)   You think about the things you've done before that remind you that you can do this.

You've got a math test that is fifty questions long and you've got two hours to do it. What do you do to motivate yourself to get this task done?

(a)   Sit for an hour not doing anything, then rush to get the test done.

(b)   Tell yourself that you can do this and that when you are done, you will reward yourself with a well-deserved candy bar.

(c)   Pull the pigtails of the girl who sits in front of you.

Chapter 5

How to Develop Rapid Reading Skills

'Not everything that can be counted counts, and not everything that counts can be counted.' – Albert Einstein

It's not likely that you have lived this long and not heard of speed reading. There are many courses that boast about having you reading seven books or more each week by the end of their – sometimes – expensive courses. You shouldn't believe everything you hear or read.

The average reading speed for a schooled reader is between 200 and 400 words per minute. Anything over 400 words per minute will mean you've lost some of the comprehension about the material you've just spent time reading. You don't want to do that.

So let me tell you about how we read. We use our eyes. Duh. I know. But how we do that isn't a thing that everyone knows. We have three phases of sight when reading. We see what's right in front of us and that's called fixation and that is in our foveal line of vision. Off to either side of that line is our parafoveal line of vision. And of course, you've heard of peripheral vision, which is off to both sides even further and a little on the blurry side.

Our eyes don't move back and forth smoothly while reading. They move in jerky movements. And when a word is long, or new to us, we become fixated on it until our brains either understand it or give up and tell us to research that cluster of letters to find out what it means and how its pronounced.

Now as fast as our eyes are moving over words that doesn't mean we're taking each word in. There are words that are important to the concept. These words are called content words. They make up what's important about what we're reading.

The other words, words we tend to skip over are called function words. These words as like filler words, the, and, if, but, those kinds of words. If we skip too many of these words, we still might not understand the concept words.

Our brains can only handle about four things at a time. And if these things are new to us, then we can only handle smaller amounts of the information at a time. Trying to push large amounts of new information into our brains isn't easy and it won't help anyone learn faster. It will actually slow the learning process down.

When you have to go back over material again and again because your brain failed to receive that information, it slows learning down. If information was put in too fast and not enough of the concept words made it into the cognitive process your brain does on its own, then you will be forced to read everything again. That just wastes time.

Why not do it once and do it right. Speed reading is cool, but if you speed past pertinent information, then you've missed the boat, so to speak.

Staying within the 200 to 400 word per minute range will help your cognitive process keep up with your reading speed. Both things are necessary when trying to learn new things.

You might get by with reading faster than 400 words per minute if you are familiar with the subject at hand. If this is completely new information to you, take the time to read it and take it in so your brain can accept the information and catalogue it where it needs to go inside your head.

Like anything else, we get faster and better at it with practice. Reading is just like anything else, do it enough and you will not only get faster at it, you will get better at it too.

It's pretty hard not to read at least a little each day. With texting, most of us at least read what others send to us. And with social media we read too. This is great, but we need to read more than short bursts of information to keep sharp and move forward.

What this means is that we need to read pages of words often. That way we are exercising our brains, building them up, keeping them strong and healthy too.

Now what we read often matters too. We can't expect our brains to get all muscular by reading books that are low-level reading material. We've got to read things with complex wording and varied concepts as well. Make our brains think, wonder, imagine, these are the keys to not only reading faster, but understanding new things easier.

Purposely choosing difficult reading material is an exercise that will strengthen your eyes and our brain. Your eyes will learn to recognize words it hadn't before. Your eyes are part one, your brain is part two. And together they can work to help you read and learn faster.

As you read more and pick diverse subjects to read about, you will strengthen your vocabulary. Knowing a lot of words, what they mean and how to use them correctly as well as how to pronounce then correctly is a thing one gains from reading often. You gain a lot when you read!

Staying interested in what you're reading can be a challenge. If you can pick out your own reading material, try to find things that interest you. Try to find things that pertain to things that interest you. If you like to play video games, then you might want to read something that has the something to what that game does.

Sometimes we get bored while reading and it's not the subject matter at all. It might very well be where you're reading. If reading in your bedroom bores you, read at the library or at a restaurant or coffee shop. Mix it up if it's not working for you. No one says there's only one place to read.

When you get a new book, even a text book, read the chapter headings first. Get to know what is in this new book. Get your brain ready to accept what's in the new book.

If there are questions at the end of chapters, read them before you read the chapter. This way you will know what to be looking for while reading. It makes sense if you really think about it.

Knowing what to look for makes your brain aware and ready to respond. Think if it as priming your mind. Setting up the hurdles that will come and being prepared for them is key to reading something once and learning it.

Once you've got those questions in your mind, you might skim over the pages to find words that match words in the questions. This will help you find the answers more quickly and make the learning process shorter.

Speed reading is only as good as what you do with the knowledge you've gained from it. Can you use any of what you read to think about your life or anything you're doing or have done?

Don't merely let the words go in one eye and out the other. Take them in, nourish them, grow them. Take the ideas that came along with what you read and see what you can do with them. How could you explain what you read to someone else in a different way than the writer did? How can you make what you've read, your own?

And why would you want to?

Knowing how to take information that you obtain and turn it into your own words and work is a necessity. In your classes, you will be asked to research different topics. From that research, information gathered by others and put into an article, book, or report, you will make your own report. This document that you make cannot be made up of the exact words of anything you've read. This is why it's of the utmost importance that you not only learn what you're reading, but you also learn how to make that information your own.

Now let's really think about what speed reading is. Is it the fact that you can say you ready three or more books in one week? Is it about the fact that you can point to your bookcase and gloat about how many books are on there that you've actually finished reading? Or is it about what you can say that you have truly learned from what you've read?

I'd rather be able to say that I've learned more in the last week than I've learned in a month's time. The number of books one reads in a week makes no difference to me nor anyone else, really.

So what's all the hoopla about speed reading?

It is just that – hoopla.

Yes, learning how to read faster is a great thing to know how to do. That means learning how to get your brain ready and primed to learn. That means knowing which words you can skim over and which words to actually read. That means knowing what the words you are reading are about.

Speed reading isn't about racing others to finish books. Speed reading isn't about seeing how fast you can get through a book. If that's what you were shooting for, then you might be able to achieve that goal. But what have you really accomplished by putting three books on your shelf with the claim that you've read them all from cover to cover?

What if someone asks you about what you've read, then what? Can you accurately answer all the questions one might throw at you?

If you take the time to read correctly, take in the content words, skim over the function words, and give your brain time for cognitive processing to work, then you will actually learn something.

If you take the time to think about what you've read, you will actually be able to put that information into your very own words. Repeating what you've read, verbatim won't be necessary.

Want to know why that is?

Because you have really learned the material you read about. You didn't merely look at some of the words, think you got what the writer was shooting for, and put the book down. No, you took the time to let all that knowledge sink into your brain. When you do that, you have that embedded in your memory. You won't easily forget what you've read. And you will be smarter for that.

Okay, so what have we learned in this chapter?

What words in these sentences are content words?

Mary rode her bike to school on Saturday.

Are the content words:

    (a)   Rode, to, on
    (b)   Mary, bike, school, Saturday
    (c)   Mary rode her bike

I like ice cream on a warm, sunny day.

Are the content words:

    (a)   Ice cream is good

    (b)   I, ice cream, day

    (c)   Warm, sunny, like

If you have to read something over again because you read it too fast before what is that called?

    (a)   Repetitive process

    (b)   Regression

    (c)   Religion

What is the most direct line of vision called?

    (a)   Straight

    (b)   Foveal

    (c)   Peripheral

What is more important?

    (a)   Getting more books read in a week than anyone else.

    (b)   Learning what you've read, no matter how long it took to read it.

    (c)   Being the best of the best at all times.

Chapter 6

How to Master the Art of Taking Smart Notes

'A man should look for what is, and not for what he thinks should be' – Albert Einstein.

Taking great notes isn't just about listening to a lecture and writing down what you think is pertinent. First, you must prepare yourself for the upcoming lecture.

How do you do this, you ask?

You skim over or even read entirely what the lecture will be over. Sure, this may seem redundant to you, but it's not. No lecturer can go over every aspect of what the text has in it. But you can read the text first to get the gist of the subject. Then, when you hear the words coming out of someone's mouth, you can gain more understanding of that subject. Plus, you will know better what you need to take note of and what you already understand well enough not to bother with.

For instance, let's say that you are already well versed in the subject of conjugating verbs. You don't need to hear or read another word about that. But what you don't know a thing about is dissecting sentences. So, you will want to take notes on that. By reading about the subject first, listening to someone talk about it next, then writing it down, third, you will cement that into your brain.

Before you head off to the lecture hall, make sure you've got what you will need to take great notes. You will need your laptop in some instances. You will always need pens and/or pencils. Highlighters are always a great idea to have too. What else would you need to bring with you?

How about paper, or a notepad? How about headphones to listen to music if you get bored? Nah!

You need to be ready to listen intently to the lecturer. If you go in with a bored attitude, you can't expect to get much out of what anyone says. Plus, you won't care about taking notes that will help you learn the material that is being gone over. What a huge waste of time and if your parents are paying for your classes, then you're wasting money too.

Now onto sustenance while in the lecture hall. Coffee is considered the old standby. But caffeine can do things to your body and brain that don't automatically mean that you will have the best concentration.

Try taking a bottle of water, instead of a giant mocha latte with double espresso shots and the sugar content of an entire chocolate cake. Water will keep you hydrated and not focusing on how dry your mouth is and how much longer you have to be in the lecture hall. Plus, it won't affect your mood, your body's ability to sit still, nor your brain's ability to pay attention. It's a win, win, win!

Before you go into the lecture hall, make sure you've put something sustainable into your stomach. You don't want to start daydreaming of pizza while trying to focus.

Leave the sugary snacks out. Put something that will last into your belly. Nuts, fruits, cheeses, and lean meats are best. Put a snack together and eat it before getting into your class or lecture hall. There are even plenty of snack options you can find at the store that include everything you need for something with protein, carbs, and the right kinds of fats to help curb that appetite for a while. And your tummy won't growl embarrassingly either.

Now we're back to mindset – see I told you it was important!

If you're in a foul mood, you know, the dog barked all night and you're going on no sleep, then you won't do well. It's important to get good rest before dealing with your day, if you want it to be productive.

If the dog's barking, do what you can to stop it. If you can't stop it, say it's the neighbor's dog, then do what you can to obliterate that noise. Even if you turn on some white noise to block it out, do what you have to, so that you can get the rest you need.

The important thing here is to get into the right mindset. Attitude is everything!

Okay, so you've got a good night's sleep. You ate a healthy, filling snack too. You didn't consume any coffee or other caffeine, so you're chill, loose, relaxed and have your bottle of water handy. Your backpack has all the essentials you will need and you, my friend, are ready to rock.

You get into the lecture hall or the classroom, you take your seat, get out your pad of paper and a pen and are keen on learning more about this subject you have read up on. And right off the bat, you notice that the lecturer touches on something he'd touched on in a prior lecture.

What do you do?

Should you ignore what he's said? He did say it already, after all.

No way. If it's important enough for him to reiterate it, then you had better write that down. Anything that is repeated might very well be important, so keep your ears open for repetition and write it down, even if you have in previous notes.

Structuring your notes is key. There are different ways to do this, so pick what works best for you.

Outlining your notes might work best for you, it does for many people.

You would do this by reading the material ahead of time and making an outline of it. Check out the key points in the text and put them in your outline, there should be four or five of these key points most of the time.

Under these key points, leave space to add in what the lecturer has to say on them. You can take notes this way on paper or on a computer, whatever is easier for you.

Another method is called the Cornell Method. In this way you will use paper to take your notes. First, you will divide your paper into three parts. Make a line down the left side to block off a small portion. Leave the right side larger. Then, at the bottom, draw a line all the way across. On the left side you will write the cues – these would be the key points of the text the lecturer is going over. On the right side, you will write the notes. On the bottom you will write the summary of the whole lecture. Most lectures summarize at the end anyway, making this easier for you to know what to write.

What if you don't do well with notes like that?

Then you can do what is called a mind map. This consists of cartoon-like bubbles that you write information in. Again, it's just like the other way of taking notes, only more visual.

There are still key points, you will put these in their own bubbles. Off to the sides of these key points, you will either draw a line to another bubble or you will overlap the bubbles to show that what you've written goes with that key point.

As you can see, every type of note taking has some sort of an outline to start with. This is an important part of the note taking process.

If you haven't reviewed the material to be covered in the lecture – shame on you. But it happens, right?

Flow notes are okay – not great, not advised – but you've got to do something. Just write down what jumps out at you with flow notes. Draw little doodles of things if you want, make smaller notes below larger texts if you need to. But keep in mind that studying these types of notes later on isn't easy.

Are you a visual learner more so than anything else?

Bullet Journaling might be best for you. It's graphic, still uses the same concept of an outline, but makes it more eye-catching.

You have your key points. Then beside them, you've got bullet points where you jot down the notes that go with those points. It's much easier to study off these types of notes too whether you're a visual learner or not.

The fact is that different subject warrant different ways to take notes. While history might work better with mind mapping notes, and English lecture might be better if taken in the Cornell method. Make sure the subject matches the way you take notes.

Lastly, let's go over whether you should take notes on your computer or write then down on paper. Some studies have been done on this controversy. What is known to be true is that students who use their computers to take notes tend to type in everything the speaker says. When tested later, they didn't retain as much of the information as students who wrote down the notes on paper.

The reason behind this is that the brain processes information better as we write it down, rather than listening and simply transcribing the lecture.

So, what have we learned?

Is there more than one way to take notes?

    (a)   True
    (b)   False

Is there only one right way for each person to take notes?

    (a)   True
    (b)   False

Will a visual learner take better notes than someone who learns better by listening?

(a)   Yes
(b)   No

Should you take notes the same way for every subject?

    (a)   Of course
    (b)   No, there are different styles that work best with certain subjects

When taking notes should you load up on sugar and caffeine?

    (a)   Why not?
    (b)   No way.

Is it important to pre-read the material before coming to a lecture?

    (A)   Why would I do that? The teacher is going to tell me everything I will need to know?
    (B)   I should always read the material before going to lecture so I will be able to understand it better and give my brain more opportunities to comprehend it.

Is getting a good night's sleep important for what you're doing the next day?

    (A)   Not at all. What does one day have to do with another?
    (B)   Yes, it matters a lot.

What is better for you; water or coffee?

(a)   Water

(b)   Coffee

(c)   Straight sugar

Chapter 7

How to Memorize Like an Elephant

'A ship is always safe at shore but that is not what it's built for.' – Albert Einstein

With our brains memorizing things in three different ways, it's not a wonder we need to know how each way works.

Sensory register is on way the brain memorizes This means that you take in things with your senses. And what are your senses?

Smell, touch, taste, sight, and sound are your five senses. You can take in information with each sense. Let's say that you're walking along in Central Park in New York City. There are lots of things that your senses can take in and that you will make memories out of.

The smell of hotdogs cooking on a food cart. The way the ground feels under your bare feet. The way that hotdog tastes when you take the first bite of it. The sight of skyscrapers against a blue sky. And the sound of cars honking as they try to navigate the busy streets.

If you've ever been to New York or any other huge city, then you can vividly recall most things you experienced there.

Another way to memorize is through your working memory. This type of memory may not last long but it can get you through until you are able to jot down the information.

You're in the elevator. It stops at a floor and someone steps inside. You know them. It's Kayla from high school. You reach into your pocket but you've forgotten your cell phone on your desk upstairs. You don't even have a piece of paper or a pen. But you want to get her number. You'd like to meet up later to catch up. What can you do?

When Kayla tells you what her phone number is, you can repeat it a couple of times out loud, then say it silently inside your head. You may have to say it out loud all the way to your office before you can write it down. You have successfully kept it in your memory for the amount of time you needed to.

Now let's take that short-term memory of Kayla's phone number and see if we can make it into one that you will have long-term.

You call Kayla later that night. The two of you go out. You connect like never before. You and Kayla end up dating. You fall in love. And all of a sudden you realize that you've got her number in your long-term memory.

Even after you broke up and years have passed, you still have her number buried in your brain. Even if you wanted to forget it and her, you can't. It's there, stuck.

Now that you know the three different ways that we memorize things, it's time to see what kinds of techniques are out there to help us memorize.

The method of Loci is one way to memorize. Loci is Latin for places. I bet you've already got a good idea of how this technique works.

Visualization is key to this technique. You will visualize a place, such as your school. You want to remember where your English class is. There are three hallways when you enter the building. So, the building is the place you will recall first. Then you will see yourself in the entrance, taking the hallway that leads to your English class. Mrs. Stainer is in the class, smiling at you as you enter. And you have successfully remembered where the class is and now it's stored in your long-term memory vault.

Another technique is the Mnemonic Peg System. This is where you put together a list and number the items on it. One – let the dog out each morning. Two – put the dog's food in his bowl and place it on the same spot on the floor each day so he can find it. Three – leave the doggy door unblocked, so he can get out to use the bathroom while you're gone. Four- if you forget any of these steps, your dog will go hungry and use the bathroom in your home. Now, this is stored in your long-term memory.

Not only will you remember these steps for your current pet, you will remember them for all the pets that come after this one. You will never have to relearn this bit of information as long as you live.

As you can see from the techniques above, we have an easier time storing smaller amounts of information into our memory banks at a time. Given time, the information builds up and then you have a lot of it stored.

How can you use this in your daily struggle to learn?

Easy.

You've got vocabulary words in most classes that you have. Take five words each day and write them down as well as the definitions of them. Each day, you will add five more words to your list. And each day you will reread the ones you wrote the previous day. Little by little, you will incorporate all of the words into your mind, your vocabulary, and your long-term memory bank.

Using the Peg System to make lists, you will make these lists in some of your classes. In history class you may need to memorize dates of major battles in the Korean War. List them in order of when they happened. Visualize that list each day when you first get into your history class. By the end of that week, you should have that information stored away right where it belongs – in your long-term memory.

Our brains are hard-wired to forget things that don't matter to us. If you meet a room full of people and have no reason to recall any of their names as you will doubtfully ever meet again, you won't even attempt to memorize anyone's name. On the other hand, if you are joining a group and will work long-term with them, it will be important to you to recall their names. You will keep repeating the names of the people out loud and silently, inside your mind.

Why?

Because it's important to you. Your brain only has so much space. If what is seen, heard, or read isn't important, the brain won't even try to store that information. It will go in one ear and out the other with ease.

Memorizing isn't as easy. That is why we have developed techniques. Loci helps you remember places and what is in those places. The Peg system helps you create lists in your mind. You can merge to two techniques when you need to, to make more in-depth memories.

Associative learning techniques, people, place, and location association go along with the Loci method of memorizing. You recall a place, and the location of that place, and who all is in that place. You also recall what is inside that place – desks, chairs, blackboard – those kinds of things.

While visiting a place, let's say our local library, you are practicing active learning. You are actively learning where the library is. You are learning what the building looks like. And you are learning what's inside of this building. And you're doing it all without even having to try to memorize it at all.

The phonetic number system is essential in the Peg System because you rely on using numbers to remember things. Using numbers is a key way to memorize all sorts of things.

Memory palaces refers to places with tons of memories inside. One can think of your lifetime of memories as a palace. There are so many memories that they can't be shut into one home or one building. We make an entire palace in our minds to store those vast amounts of memories.

Using stories to aid memories is another way we can memorize things. In history for example, you can make a story out of the events. This helps you not only visualize the material, but it can help you store this information in various ways too.

As you tell or read a story or even watch one, you almost live that life along with the characters. That's why we cry along with the characters of a story or laugh with them or even love with them. We become part of that story and as a part of it, we retain memories of what occurred.

Now let's see what we've learned about memorizing that will help us become accelerated learners, shall we?

You've got an important math test, what can you do to make sure you remember the equations that will be on the test?

(a)   Use Loci to store that information.

(b)   Use the Mnemonic Peg System

(c)   Use your fingers and toes.

You are going to your first day at a new school. How are you going to remember where your classes are?

(a)   Use a marker to write on the walls to tell you where to go.

(b)   Use the Loci System

(c)   Use the Mnemonic Peg System.

You are about to meet some new people that you will be expected to team up with to make a project. How can you remember their names?

(a)   You can put a number to each name and make a mental list.

(b)   You can ask them to wear nametags.

(c)   You can write on their forehead with a marker so you will never forget their name.

Your great grandmother is in the hospital and she's going to be there for a week. You want to visit every day, but the place is huge and you're having a hard time remembering where her room is. What can you do to put this into your memory?

(a)   Nothing, it's hopeless. You just won't see her until she goes back home.

(b)   You can start by walking into the hospital and making a mental map of the place. This will help store the information into your long-term memory bank.

(c)   You can bake her a pie and hope it takes her a week to eat it because you could never remember how to get around that place.

Visualizing scenes, making up stories, and putting things you need to remember on mental lists are all ways to recall important things.

(True)

(False)

You can use different methods as ways to store information in your long-term memory.

(yes)

(no)

Having ways to remember things isn't important with today's technology.

(True)

(False)

Chapter 8

How to Properly CRAM

'Education is not the learning of facts, it's rather the training of the mind to think.' – Albert Einstein

The old ways of cramming for an exam are long gone – well, if you actually want to ace the test, that is.

Our brains don't automatically take in everything we want them to. One cannot read five chapters an hour or even the night before an exam and hope to make a good grade. Our brains learn better with something called spaced repetition.

Think of this the same way you would think of a way of strengthening any muscle in your body. Say you'd like some awesomely buff abdominal muscles. So you do a thousand sit ups then magically see the ladder of defined muscles appear on your tummy?

You wish!

No, you do twenty sit ups on day one. Twenty more the next day, maybe add five more. Do the same amount the next day and increase the number again. Over and over you will do this and a few weeks later you are actually looking at what your work did for you.

The same concept goes for learning. Cramming sounds effective, but it's not, if done the old-fashioned way.

When you cram too many clothes into your washing machine, not only will your clothes not get as clean as you'd like them too, your washer might even break. The same goes for your brain.

When you try to input too much new information into your brain, you might get brain-fry. This is a real thing, guys. I'm sure you've all experienced this at one time or another.

Think about semester exams. If every single one of your classes had the tests on the same day, then you would surely suffer from a severe case of brain-fry. One cannot possibly store eight classes of information in a place where it can be easily retrieved back.

Never fear though, there is a way to effectively cram that will have you acing your tests. When you space out the repetition of studying, you actually make that information stick better.

Start working on this as many days in advance as you can. At the least, a few days. Take an hour each day to read over your notes. On day two, read them once, then give it a few hours and read them again. Day three, add in a third time when you read your notes, make sure to give yourself hours in between these times.

Giving your brain breaks to think about other things is key to spaced repetition. Much like we talked about how to remember a phone number very short term, if you try to remember the notes you have for a test by reading them over and over, back to back, you will see that they haven't stuck.

We need neural connections to form in some cases. When your tests require you to use analysis, then you have to have a vast amount of information stored in your brain to do this.

If all you can recall are small parts of the whole, you can effectively analyze anything. So you must take your time and space out the reading of the notes and text that you need to not only know but understand.

The old brick wall idea comes into play here. You've got a brick wall to build. Can it be done in one day? Can the mortar between the layers of brick dry effectively if one layer of bricks is put on top of another before the mortar on the first layer has had time to dry at least a little bit?

We've all seen warped brick walls. Just looking at the shoddy work tells us it was put up way too fast. And like anything that's full of holes and leaning over, it will fall. All of that hard work will be for nothing. The wall will have to be built all over again.

What are you out if that happens?

Time, money, and energy are all expended to replace the wall. If you would've just slowed the pace, then it would've lasted forever. That's a fact you can see in ancient structures that have been around for thousands, and thousands of years.

Rome wasn't built in a day, is a popular euphemism to explain how good things take time. Learning takes time. Cramming foils the plan. Letting your brain have access to the information needed to actually learn a lesson is not only important, it's necessary.

Our brains have what is called storage strength and retrieval strength. If something is important to us, we keep it in storage – close at hand. Think of it like you would your favorite pair of jeans. You store them at the front of the closet. You like to wear them a lot and don't want to have to go searching for them.

Now think about where you store your winter coat. You don't wear this every day. You only use it once a year. So you don't keep it in the front of your closet. You keep in the back or maybe even in another closet altogether. You must retrieve this item if you want to use it.

Memory is the same way. You know right off the bat what date your birthday is on. You know that because even though it only happens once a year, it's important to you.

Uncle Joe's birthdate might even be on the same day as yours is. Chances are that you don't recall that at all. Why?

Well, you don't celebrate that day as his day. You consider that to be your special day. Although, somewhere in the back of your mind, you know that Uncle Joe and you share a birthdate, it's not at the forefront.

When we have tests to take, we use some of each kind of memory. Some of it is right there, important to us. Other aspects of it have to be searched for, left in the dark depths of information that barely matters to us and we only need it on occasion.

Still, the memory is still there, we just have to retrieve it is all. And that takes some time, doesn't it?

That is exactly why you can't rush through a test, putting down what you know and leaving what you can't think of right away out. Take your time on tests. Give your brain a chance to retrieve some of the information stored in the recesses of your mind.

The space you've given your mind as you took in the information is thick. Don't rush yourself. Let your mind meander through the layers to get to what you need.

Forgetting some things is healthy for the brain. The same way that any other muscle in your body is flexed, built up, and then sometimes let go so other muscles can be worked on, the brain needs times of rest too. It needs to let some things go to work on others.

When you need to think about what's been forgotten, you will find a kernel of memory left. On top of that, more grows, making it heartier. Out of that forgotten memory, a healthy one can grow.

Thanks to technology, it's easier than ever to practice spaced repetition. There are apps and websites that you can use to help you with what you need to learn for a test. All you have to do is look it up and help is there for you in a way older generations didn't have.

My advice is to use this technology, but to use the old ways as well. You never know, one day you might not have access to a computer or a cell phone to help you with what you need to remember.

While having a host of ways to learn and remember is like a gift from above, knowing what the basics are will serve you better in the long run. That way you know more than one way to do what you need to do.

Answer these questions to help you better understand how to cram for a test.

The teacher has told you on Monday that you will have a test on Friday. Do you take out your notes and give them the once over? Or do you chillout, as you feel confident that you know the material and won't need to study at all?

Do you believe that confidence is better than having the insurance of reading over what will be on the test?

If you have more than one day to study for a test, should you space out the time you look over the notes or should you read them last minute and hope you make a passing grade?

Is it more important to you to make merely a passing grade on an exam or is it more important that you learn the material you are being tested on?

If you have to build a dog house out of bricks, should you try to do it all in a couple of hours?

What might happen if you stack the bricks too high before the mortar that glues them together dries?

Will your dog be safe in a brick doghouse that you built in an hour?

What could happen to your dog if your doghouse fails and falls apart?

Is forgetting things healthy for your brain?

When you have seemingly forgotten something, do you think that learning about it again can build and even strengthen what you once knew?

If you are making a cake and you toss all of the ingredients in at the same time then toss them into the oven will you end up with the type of cake you desire?

Why is it important to take one step at a time when doing most things?

(a)   Everything needs a proper and sturdy foundation.
(b)   Nothing can be done right if you eliminate the steps.
(c)   Cramming things together doesn't mean they will stay put together.

(d)   All of these things are correct.

In conclusion of this chapter- the brain is a complex organ that is sometimes called a muscle. But it isn't a muscle at all. It is the most important organ of all and it controls muscles.

We use the euphemism of muscle to gain a better understanding of how our brains can become stronger by learning new things and testing our memories. This is to make a mental picture of what is happening inside of our heads, much like exercising makes a difference in how our muscles appear and how strong they are.

Using visuals can help us learn and recall things better than just listening or reading about things. Combining how we intake information is important for the learning process. Using combinations helps accelerate the learning process.

Chapter 9

Show What You Know

'I have no special talent. I am only passionately curious.' – Albert Einstein

Some teachers allow the students to take turns teaching the lessons. Why do they do this?

It's not to make their job easier, if that's what you're thinking.

When one teaches what they have learned, it further cements that knowledge into their brains. It does so even better than taking a test does. So knowing how to share the things we've learned is really important.

There are various ways to share knowledge. One can write a paper about a subject they've mastered. One could write an entire book about it. The main thing is to share what we've learned with others.

You never know when what you know might help someone to finally get it.

I have to go back to my high school days when I took algebra and just didn't get it. The teacher couldn't help me. No one else in the class could help me understand it. I thought I was a real idiot. I mean, it seemed like everyone but me understood algebra.

Luckily, there were two other girls in my class who were like me. So, I knew that we all couldn't be idiots. There was the fact that we all did well in other subjects. We all knew something the teacher nor our classmates knew – we had to learn this subject a different way.

Now, if no one had ever taken the time to show us what they had found out, then we may have never passed that dang algebra test. None of us would have ever gone to college. None of us would've ever amount to anything.

And all because a select few refused to share with us what they knew.

Thankfully, there were people who knew what would help us. And thankfully for others like us, we all took what we learned and helped others to understand that demon called algebra too.

I went from the Dumbo in algebra class, to the Rockstar who knew it all. As if a switch had been turned on in my head, it all started coming to me. And that was all because of how one man explained it to me.

He communicated his knowledge through the blackboard. That's one way to do it. Nowadays we use whiteboards, and you could too. Presenting information can be done in many ways.

You can make a video, or even write a song that will help people learn what you have. You can make a slideshow. Each slide could have different information that would help people learn about the subject you've aced.

Public speaking is a great thing to practice and get comfortable with. Why not make a lecture and talk about what you've learned, how you learned it, and what that knowledge can do for you and others?

Being that there are multiple people who might be having trouble with a subject, you could put together a learning group. Heading that group would mean that you would have to put your brain to work to make sure each individual understood the material completely.

Doing something like this not only helps others, but it will help you too. It will help you have empathy for others. Understanding that they are having a problem understanding or retaining the information they are given will help you connect with other people. Knowing how to help them will make you a more compassionate person.

When working with a group, you will encounter different personalities. Not only that, but you will have to deal with their individual ways of learning, which might not all be the same. You will have to help each one of them use the types of learning and memorization that works best for them.

By teaching others, you will learn more about subjects and yourself. Knowing how to teach is important. Understanding how people learn is key to this process.

You can't go into presenting what you know without doing a fair amount of research. You don't want to come to the table ill-prepared. You want to impress both your teacher and your classmates. And in the end, you will have impressed yourself as well.

Making your presentation, using more than one way is a great idea as well. The same you must incorporate different ways of learning and memorizing, you must incorporate different ways of presenting information.

Think about anything you've ever learned. How about watching a video about a subject? What all was combined in that video to teach you?

First, you've got to get people's attention. Most videos begin with music. You might have to make some music of your own for this, which can be both fun and stimulating, creatively speaking.

So, you've got the music, now you need some jaw dropping visuals, right?

You can search the web for some or you can video your own. With your cell phone, you've always got a camera with you. Now you need to gather the information you want to share with your class or group.

There are so many components and as you find what you need, you will also gain admiration and respect for your teachers, knowing how much time and effort they all put into teaching you and your classmates.

Respecting your teachers will not only make you a better student, that will accelerate your learning process even more. When you can understand what all it took to get together that information to help you learn something, you tend to pay more attention to it.

Think of it like this. When people make a movie, there are award they can receive in all categories of that process. Why is that?

Because, it's hard work.

As you put together your presentation, no matter how small, you will have to put work into it. And when you set out to present your project to people, you will want them to pay attention to what you've put out there for them. You will expect them to take some time to watch and listen to what you have to say and to show them.

You put lots of time and effort into this, so you have certain expectations of those who will benefit from it. And the people who are watching you have expectations too.

When people give you their time, they expect you to have your facts straight. They also expect you to present your facts in a timely manner. Their time is as precious to them as yours it to you. Make sure that you don't drone on or put things into your presentation that don't fit or make sense.

People think of their time as important, don't waste it. Make sure you are ready to roll when it's time to make your presentation.

And if you want to make some questions at the end of the presentation be sure you have the correct answers. If no one can answer the questions you've asked, be sure that you can.

Nothing is worse than not having the answers to your own questions.

The size of your audience makes a difference in how you want to demonstrate what you've learned as well. If there are only a couple of people in your group, you might want to do a smaller presentation.

Why make an entire video for three people?

Think about how effective your presentation will be. If you're doing a slideshow, how many slides will you need? Will you be able to effectively show people what you've learned and teach them by using slides?

It does matter how you present what you've learned. If you learned how to build a doghouse, then you might want to do a step by step class on how to do that. Using a slide show might work, but so would doing the job in front of the group. Much the way chefs have cooking shows, showing people the techniques they've mastered to prepare great food, you can show people how to make a stellar doghouse. In the end, people could come up to take a closer look at what you've done and ask questions to help them understand how to build one on their own.

Sharing what you've learned is the best way to pay back that teacher who shared what they knew to help you. Nothing makes a teacher happier than knowing what they did will go forward into the future for generations to come.

So, what have you learned from this chapter?

If you have knowledge of how to do a complex mathematical problem, what is the best way to show others how to do it?

(a)   Make a movie about it

(b)   Do an hour long lecture on it.

(c)   Use a chalkboard or a whiteboard to do the problem in front of the class or group and explain each step you did while taking questions from those who don't understand.

You did a report on exports from India that won an award. What is the best way to let people know what you now know?

(a)   Share your award winning paper with the class

(b)   Write a song about it

(c)   Give a lecture about it

(d)   Both a and c

Sharing what you know with others is not only nice, it's key to gaining an even deeper understanding of the subject matter.

(True)

(False)

If you don't have a strong grasp in the subject, should you do a presentation anyway?

(a)   Sure, who's going to know if you don't know what you're talking about anyway?

(b)   Wasting people's time isn't at thing I care about, so I don't need to know much about what I'm presenting.

(c)   If I don't have a strong grasp on a subject, I will not make a presentation about it until I do.

Chapter 10

Getting Things Done

'Life is like riding a bicycle. To keep your balance you must keep moving.' – Albert Einstein

Like most things, there's a place where you must begin if you want to get a job done quickly. Knowing what to start with when gathering information for the subject you've been tasked with, is step one. You have to know what things comes first, second, third, and so on.

Without knowing what order you need to put your tasks in, you will have more trouble understanding how to put your thoughts and knowledge in order. The best idea is to thoroughly read the material that explains what is expected for the project. Noting the most important aspects and putting them in order as the material states them is the best idea.

A popular principle of learning is the Pareto principle. The theory is that for twenty percent of what's put in, one will an output of eighty percent. In short, if you are given reading material of a couple of pages, this will give you enough input to make a report of forty percent more information than what you were initially given.

This is because we can take the smaller amounts of information and expand on them. Think of what it's like to have a conversation about something. One of the members of a group brings up a topic. That's about a sentence or two. Another person in the group adds a few more sentences to the topic. Now you've got the equivalent of one paragraph.

With this amount of information, you now have enough to make your own response, using what they gave. You can take that twenty percent and make eighty percent out of it. And you can do this because your brain can expand what you've learned.

Most people drift around when doing a task. They may start on part, then stop and go to a completely different part. Use the task of sweeping and mopping your house.

If you set up SMART goals, then you would decide to sweep the entire house first, starting in the main room then moving from that room to the next, then to the next, and on and on until the house is all swept.

Next, you would make your mop water then mop in the same way you swept. Now this is setting up SMART goals.

But some people won't think to do this task this way. Some people might want to sweep the kitchen then mop it. Then sweep their bedroom and their bathroom, then mop them. With things not going in order, most people will stop there and forget about the rest of the house. This doesn't get the whole job done.

It's important to set up your goals in a way that will see a job through to the very end. Otherwise, you end up with jobs half done and that means bad things if you're getting paid to do these jobs.

If you're getting graded on a paper that you've set no SMART goals for, you can guess what that means for your grade. Making goals for the paper is important if you want to not only pass but learn something too.

Why do an assignment if you're not going to take something away from it? Why not take every opportunity you have to learn something when given the opportunity to? In the end, you will end up with more stored knowledge, making subsequent classes easier for you.

Many people have been faced with a huge mess as some time or another and had no idea where to start cleaning. The same can be said for large assignments that seem too big to even know where to start. Just like the mess you must clean, you have to find a place to start for the assignment too.

Looking at the smallest thing first might seem smart, but it's not. Take out the large chunks of work first, then the smaller items that are left, don't seem so big and unsurmountable. Plus, getting the larger chunks done first means you've used your time wisely and gotten the major part out of the way. This means those little things can be done with the time you've got left over.

Using SMART goal setting isn't only a great idea, it's the quickest way to get done with any task you have. And who doesn't like to get work out of the way so they can play?

When using both SMART goal setting and the Pareto principle, one can make short work out of even the longest project. Your first goal is to find the material you will need to read and research to get the answers you will need. The next goal is to put that information in an order that makes sense. The goal after that is to put your mind to work, making the material you have into even more material. And finally, you will put all of this down in writing, either with pen and paper or on a computer.

Now let's do that same task without using the SMART goal setting guide not the Pareto principle. You go to the library to get a few books to help you with the assignment. Now you've got three books to read. Instead of figuring out which one to read first, you just start randomly reading. You can't find what you're looking for, so you skip around in one book only to do the same in the others. You can't find anything and your aggravated.

A day later, you decide to give it another try when you find your friend has already done their assignment. You skip the books and go straight for your computer. Using the internet, you look up something about the assignment. At the side of the page, there's an ad for shoes and you like them. You go to ask your mother if you can buy them, forgetting completely about your studies.

A couple days later, you are asked to do a bit of written work on the assignment during your class. You jot down some random thoughts you have while your friend polishes his paper. Still, you haven't got enough down to even turn in to make a poor grade. In the end, you ask your friend if you can at least read his paper. From that, you make the shortest paper possible, missing key points and information to expand on the points and ideas.

You have wasted time, energy, and resources. And what is worse, you've wasted the opportunity to learn. If it were money that you had the chance to make, would you have done anything differently?

As many know later in their lives, knowledge of things means you are often paid better for having that knowledge. So everything you learn might eventually be worth money. Does that make learning from your assignments mean more to you than they typically do?

One might not think they will ever make money using algebra. One would be wrong. Calculations are used in many jobs. Having that knowledge base without having to be taught it, is worth money.

Let's say you hate English class. You despise grammar and feel that it will never matter to you. You don't mind reading, but writing is a waste of your time.

Here's the thing about that, you will have many more classes in your school career. You will have many reports that you will have to put together. That English class is the first SMART goal in your academic career. Without learning how to spell, write sentences, use proper punctuation, and grammar, you will fail all other classes.

So, now you can see how setting up SMART goals is extremely important. So let's do some exercises to see what we've learned from this chapter.

You have a three page report on the uses of soap. How much material will you need to find through research to make this report?

(a)   Seven pages

(b)   One paragraph

(c)   One page

Your mother gives you the task of cleaning the garage which is a mess. How would you get this job done as quickly as possible.

(a)   Just open the door and start throwing things away.

(b)   Make a path through the middle then take a break, this is too hard.

(c)   Set some goals that make sense then take each goal, one at a time to finish the chore.

You have a week to make a thousand word report on birds in Ohio. You're not interested in learning about this and don't care to look much into this subject. How will doing this report benefit you anyway?

(a)   By doing this report you will learn more about birds in Ohio.

(b)   By doing this report, you will get some experience using the Pareto principle

(c)   By doing this report, you will gain experience using SMART goal setting.

(d)   You will gain all of this and even more.

If you have a paying job, and are asked to clean the parking lot of the grocery store you work at, what types of things that you've learned in school can help you with this job?

(a)   Problem solving skills.

(b)   Pareto Príncipe

(c)   SMART goal setting

(d)   Nothing from school will help me clean the parking lot at my job.

When given the opportunity to learn should you look at is as a gift or a punishment? And why?

Is learning ever a thing that you feel like is good for you?

Do you hate going to school? If so, why? If not, why?

If learning is a thing you hate, then learning to accelerate your learning speed can make it into something you actually like to do. Do you feel like this book has helped you understand that there are techniques available to you to help you learn faster?

If you have the opportunity to learn just for the fun of it, would you do it?

Do making good grades matter to you as much as learning about things?

Do you think that setting SMART goals would work for you in more ways than just school work?

Einstein has said many great things. In your opinion, which one of his quotes makes the most sense to you?

Do you think that listening to things other people have said is beneficial to you?

If you could ask Einstein any question in the world, what would it be about?

Do you think that Einstein used something like the SMART goal setting idea to learn new things?

Setting goals makes sense, how can you use this idea to make your life easier? How can you use this idea to make other people's lives easier?

Is it important to you to not only become a faster learner yourself, but to help others do it as well?

 On a scale of one to ten how well do you understand the importance of SMART goal setting for not only your learning skills, but for your life as well?

Chapter 11

How to Get Better in Getting Better

'Once you stop learning, you start dying.' – Albert Einstein

Metacognition is a big word. And it might not be one that you've ever heard before. But I bet you've done it before. Metacognition is what you do when you are thinking about thinking.

In other words, you have an idea about something, and you start to think about how you could go about getting it done. You are thinking about thinking, using metacognition.

When you are trying to become a great learner, you use metacognition more than most people. Most things you begin to get interested in are going to go through this phase before they go into any other phase.

You might be thinking about making your own fishing pole. You might reflect on fishing poles you've used before. You might picture them in your head or even look them up on the internet. You are thinking about what you can do to make your own with things you already have.

Reflecting on things you already know is an important part of the accelerated learning process. There's no need to start from scratch on every idea when you use reflection to help you moved up in the process faster than if you wouldn't have know a thing about your subject.

If you had never baked a thing in your life, the process of baking a cake would take a lot longer then it would for someone who has baked a lot.

For instance, you would have to read each line of direction slowly to make sure you had it right and to give your brain time to process the information. An avid baker would already know what the first few steps were and take them before having to look at the directions.

Some avid bakers might nor even have to take the time to read the directions, they may already know exactly what to do to make an excellent cake in no time at all.

The more you do something, the faster you will get at it. That's due to reflecting on your previous learning experiences. The first few times we do anything, we won't be as fast as we will be later on when doing those same things.

Even tying your shoes works from reflection on your previous learning experiences. We all know how long it takes to learn to not only tie your shoes, but to do it well. Having the ability to use a part of your mind to do things faster is incredible and appreciated.

So don't waste this valuable resource. Use that ability to make tasks easier and faster. Develop faith in your ability to reflect accurately on things. Don't go through steps that you don't need to just because you lack faith in what you already know.

Knowing when to skip steps that you're sure you know is key to accelerating your learning speed. Just the way you do in speed reading, knowing what words to skim over or skip entirely makes things faster.

Anything you can do to make things go faster is a great idea for you. As I've said before, getting things done means more time for you to do other things - things you enjoy. Why not use whatever you can to make that happen for you?

The things you learn, even in school, can be used in our daily life. Spelling is one that stands out. You will always need to know how to spell, even with spellcheck to help you. It might surprise you that there are a few ways to spell certain words and some words are spelled the same but mean different things. So you've got to have good spelling skills no matter what technology throws at you.

What if you have a project at school about alligators? What if you find that you are fascinated with them?

You can take what you've learned about alligators and ask your parents if you can go on a trip to see some of them in the wild. You could introduce your family to these creatures and tell them all about how gators live in the wild. And who knows, one day you might want to work on a gator farm or work at a zoo, taking care of them. One never knows.

With knowledge, comes the ability to make choices about what you do with your life. The more knowledge you have, the more choices you have. Why not have as many choices as possible? Why not take every opportunity you get to expand your knowledge? Why not make this life something other can only dream of?

All it takes is a little work to get where you need to be. Everyone can learn in easier ways. All it takes is giving yourself the chance to learn new techniques while understanding how our brains work. Don't beat yourself up over not understanding things. Instead, make an active decision to try to learn that hard to understand subject another way. There are more ways than one to learn anything. This book should've taught you a few ways that you can make learning easier and faster for you.

Use what you've learned, not only in school, but in your everyday life. From cleaning, to building things, to doing daily chores, you can use what you've learned here to get things done faster and maybe even easier.

Learning isn't only for school. The quote I used at the beginning of this chapter states that when learning stops, dying starts. See how I made that my own?

You can make everything you read, your own. It just takes practice. And the more that you practice, the better you will become at it.

Let's do some thinking about what we've learned here in this last chapter.

When you have done a task a few times before and you want to use what you remember to help you do some of the steps, what is this process called?

    (a)   Recall procession
    (b)   Thinking it out
    (c)   Reflecting on things you already know

Metacognition is a word that means...

    (a)   Learning about learning
    (b)   Talking about talking
    (c)   Thinking about thinking

When you are thinking about thinking, what does that really mean?

(a)   I am considering things that I need to in order to make rational thoughts on a subject.

(b)   I'm bored and just running in circles in my mind.

(c)   I'm thinking about something I've never thought of before.

Conclusion

Learning is a thing one never stops doing. Being a great learner isn't a thing everyone is born with, but it is a thing we can all learn how to become.

With all the new techniques available for learning, there is no reason to stay ignorant of things others know well. Having faith in your ability to learn is important.

One may not learn in the way everyone else in a class is learning. But they can learn that same subject in other ways. All it takes is the desire to learn and a little help from someone who's had to learn things other ways to make the changes that need to be made.

Once you have learned how to learn in an alternative fashion, it's important to help others do the same. Giving back is important. It not only helps others, it helps you to become self-assured, and secure in your ability to learn things you thought you were incapable of before. Giving that to another person feels good because it is good. Sharing knowledge is a thing we were all meant to do.

When you consider the fact that not that many years ago students had a much harder time in school that you do today, it should make you appreciate what you have now. Once there were classes of children who all learned at the same speed. If you didn't learn even one subject at the speed of the rest of the class, you were sent to another class.

Going to another class where all the subjects were taught at a slower pace didn't actually help someone who only learned one subject more slowly. Being taught things you naturally understood faster than the rest of the students in the now slower learning class could become mundane. This slow learning process on other subjects would affect the child adversely. This wasn't the way to deal with learning problems.

Thankfully, people did work and found ways to help all the students find better ways to help them learn all subjects. All we have to do now is use that help that people worked so hard to give us.

You might feel shy or embarrassed about asking for help learning something that everyone else seems to be learning easily. Don't be. Don't let shyness or embarrassment stop you from gaining the knowledge everyone else has. Reach out, take the help that is out there and use it.

We all are capable of great things. We all can't do everything great, but we all can do some things great. All it takes is the want to. All it takes is the desire to succeed and the willingness to seek help to make it all happen for you.

This can be achieved. You can master things you never thought possible and you can do it faster than you ever dreamed. So don't ever give up and keep on reading, researching, and learning.

Dear reader,

I sincerely hope that you feel inspired my book and enjoyed the Do-It-Yourself Exercises.

Before you close this book I´d like you to ask to write an honest review on amazon. It´d be greatly appreciated.

Just click here to leave a review on amazon.

Thank you and till soon!

Accelerated Learning

Learn more in less time, direct your own education
and teach yourself anything with self-learning
Including DIY-exercises

By Patrick Lightman

Introduction

When I was fresh out of high school, I had no learning goals. I was sick and tired of school and all the classes, the boring lectures, the dull assignments that never seemed to make much sense for me and what I wanted to do with my life.

I had no idea what to chalk that up to back then, later on, I did. See, I didn't like the teacher-student learning process. I was more of a hands-on type of learner - more of a teach myself kind of person, and as such, I didn't cotton to classrooms.

After working for the family business, I got married, had kids, and did that kind of life for a long time. When all my children were in school all day, and I didn't have anything else to do but watch soap operas on the television all day while eating snacks, I decided I finally had time to do me.

But what did I want to do?

I'd lived my life for other people for years. I had never furthered my education since I disliked brick and mortar colleges. Plus, there still wasn't time to go to classes even if I'd wanted to with still having lots to do for my children once school got out. The endless activities that children have can take hours after school gets out. College still wasn't going to be the right thing for me.

Working when I was younger for the family business had given me the drive to try my hand at making a business of my own. I knew I could use what I'd learned from working with my family, but I wanted to do it even better than they had.

I've often been accused of being, EXTRA, whatever that means.

So, being what I was, I wanted to get an education. I didn't care if it was a few business classes or what, I wanted to know more. Luckily for me, online college had become a thing while I was in the throes of motherhood and wifedom.

Faced with many critics, naysayers who reminded me of my not so great grades back in high school, I had to overcome my fear of failing. My hubby was paying good money for my online college experience, to let him down by failing was a bit overwhelming. We weren't rich by any means. Every penny had a place, and I had to cut quite a few corners in the house budget just to get the money for my schooling.

But I did it. I ignored the negative feedback I'd gotten and only focused on my positive attitude. See, I knew something about myself that no one else did. I had a remarkable can-do spirit that I'd built within myself by being a wife and a mother.

You know that spirit. Everything seems to be against you. The baby has a diaper rash; your oldest is a teen with mood swings. And your husband has to have meatloaf every Tuesday or civilization will collapse, as far as he knows. With all that going on in one's life for years, one learns how to make things happen when it seems impossible.

Once I had to make meatloaf out of leftover hamburger patties from our son's fifth birthday party. Did my husband ever catch on? No way!

I was that good at finding a way to make things happen. So, I knew I could do the same with my online classes.

And I did just that. The college I was accepted to, gave me two classes at a time. That split the workload up for me in a way that I could handle easily with my eight hours of free time, five days a week.

I was able to fly through my courses at my own speed, which was rapid. And I not only made exceptional grades; I learned so much more than I'd learned in twelve years of contemporary schooling.

The best thing about going to online classes was that I loved learning and have never stopped. I went from having nothing more than a high school diploma for fifteen years after graduation to betting a Bachelor's Degree in Business Administration in only three years. I'd knocked a whole year off getting that degree.

I learned a lot about how to accelerate my learning, and I'd love to share what I learned with you. I want to help you achieve goals you've never thought you could have before. So, grab a bottle of water, some almonds for a snack and perhaps a pen and paper to jot down notes because I'm about to take you on a journey you won't soon forget.

Chapter 1

Why Self-Learning Beats Traditional Learning

'Success is no accident. It is hard work, perseverance, learning, studying, sacrifice and most of all, love of what you are doing or learning to do.' – Pele

Most people have little to no choice on how they begin their institutional learning years. Tradition tells us to put our children into preschool as early as three-years-old. And while most children are in day-care at least some of the workweek, they are taught from even earlier ages.

The classroom method of teaching is undeniably the best for us when we're too young to educate ourselves. At the very least, our parents and older siblings have to teach us things. Until our brains are developed enough to understand that we will have to search for the knowledge that is out there for the taking, we must depend on others to help us learn the basics.

Reading is a basic skill that is taught to us early on, as is counting. We learn how to count our fingers and toes with the help of our family. Later, in school, we learn more about numbers and counting, even how to do basic math.

If you've got these two basic skills, believe it or not, you've got all you will need in your arsenal of learning tools to get started on teaching yourself. Reading is the number one thing any person needs to know to learn everything they can. And knowing what to do with numbers is a close second.

Even if you are a horrible speller, you've still got what it takes to teach yourself. There is spell check nowadays, thank goodness.

So let's make a list of the pros and cons between traditional, classroom learning and do-it-yourself learning.

Traditional classrooms have at least one teacher in them. If there are aids, then you level the playing field at least a bit. When I was a kid, there were around thirty students in a class. Thirty to one or even three are poor odds in my opinion.

Some others must have agreed with me between the years of my schooling and the years of my children's schooling because the student to teacher ratio has gotten smaller. But the number of children who have difficulty learning in the traditional manner has risen, so we've pretty much got the same problems we've always had.

Now, there may be far more children with problems learning certain things than there were when I was young, or there may not be an increase in this at all. After all, our classes weren't what they are now. We had students who made around the same grades in the same class. If you had very little difficulty learning things, you were put into a group that learned similarly. That segregated students and made it so the students who had troubles only went to class where other students had the same troubles. This is my theory of why we think there has been an explosion in learning disorders.

They've always been there, they were just masked by making the criteria of those classes less than what was expected of the students in other classes who understood things easier. This wasn't fair to the students who were taught down to. They weren't given the opportunities to learn as much as those who had little to no difficulty learning.

Thankfully, these practices were stopped, but the way teachers have been taught to teach hasn't changed much at all. And in this lies the problem at hand. Are you a better teacher for yourself than someone trained to teach?

Will you make strides in learning if you sit in a classroom full of others? Will you learn quickly by reading a text book and listening to a teacher try to explain things to a group of people who all learn in different ways.

The first thing I did when I was accepted at the online college was take a little test. Not a test that was graded on what I currently knew. No, this test was to distinguish how I learned best.

Some people learn best by reading. Others learn best by listening or watching videos. And still others do better by learning things hands-on.

In a typical classroom, you are supposed to learn by reading. That is the main way teachers have taught in the past and in the present as well. Unless the way teachers are taught to teach changes rather drastically, the way we've always known school will never be enough for us or our future generations.

Thankfully, you won't have to wait for such huge changes to be made in our school systems. You can start learning right now, and some things you can even learn for free. Online, you can find many free courses to help you learn about things that previously you would've had to pay to learn.

This is a great time in our world. Children are learning much younger than they ever have before. Adults who thought their educational days were far behind them, never to be seen again, now have chance after chance to further their education.

The fact is, even if you are a reading learner, you can also learn by watching videos. There are so many educational videos out there, both online and on television, that you will learn much more than your parents ever did, and in record time too.

Don't worry if all you have to work with right now is traditional teaching in the public school system. You can learn more on your own anyway. With the free online classes, you don't have to get stuck in a rut with traditional learning methods. You can move past this on your own.

If you are having problems in any subject, you can bypass the regular method of learning by seeking an online way to help you understand the subject. Who cares if it was an online platform that helped you succeed? The important thing is that you did learn the subject and you did well at it too.

Grades used to be the most important thing to students and teachers. In public schools, they still are. Not only that, but the yearly state and federal testing makes it so teachers now only teach for those big tests. Students who have made passing grades all year long now aren't moved on to the next grade until they can pass the state or federal exam. How fair is this?

Not at all.

First of all, I doubt any of you want to learn anything just so you can pass a test. Knowledge isn't about that. Tests have their places, but by far it's the storage of knowledge that you've built in your brain that matters to most.

Let's say you've got this killer cake recipe. Let's say you were given a test on this recipe. Maybe the way the questions were worded confused you a bit. Maybe you didn't ace the test on your own recipe. Do you really care about that since you can still make the cake and people swarm to eat it?

Most people get a kick out of making a good grade on a test or an assignment and that's perfectly fine. But the real winning point is that you gained the knowledge and understanding in the first place. Whether you were ever tested on the subject or not, you've won just by learning.

The things that really matter in this world and to you aren't in text books, or in the grades you can make by reading them and listening to teachers say the same things year after year. Doing, thinking, feeling, and experiencing things first hand mean more than any number of hours spent in a classroom.

Back when I was in high school, my family had the chance to go to Wyoming as my father had business there. Being from Southern Texas, we'd never had the opportunity to see mountains, especially giant mountain ranges that I'd read about only in textbooks. I had the chance to see The Rocky Mountains in real life. I had the chance to see wildlife I would've never seen in real life had I not been able to take this trip.

The problem arose that the trip would take two weeks and the attendance code only allowed five days of absences in a semester. If I went, I would face the risk of not being passed to the next grade level, based on attendance alone.

I had good grades at this time, and there was no chance of my failing any of my classes, so why should attendance be a factor in my failing an entire grade level?

My parents had to fight for me to get to go on this trip and in the end, they still lost. I did go on the trip but had to pay the price when I got back home.

Although my grades were still good and I'd gotten my assignments from my teaches before leaving and turned them in on my arrival back to school, there were still repercussions I had to pay. For the remainder of the year, six months, I had to stay after school for an hour each day. At lunch, I had to go sit in a teacher's room, doing nothing. And each and every Saturday, I had to go to school, sit in a classroom with kids who had gotten into real trouble, and do nothing as I had all of my work done already.

No, traditional schooling isn't perfect or even forgiving. For this reason and loads of others, I prefer other resources for learning. Back then, I had nothing to help me, but then the information boom hit with the advance of home computers and online content.

In this day and age, no one should ever get left behind no matter what their background, age, social problems, or monetary gains. We all can get the education we want and deserve.

In this book, I will show you how to go about getting what you need and should demand. Life is short. Learning is important. You've got to take the bull by the horns. You've got to go out and get what's your for the taking.

There is no reason to sit home or sit in a classroom that is doing nothing for you. Not when you can get online and get the knowledge you crave. Not when there is so much out there for you. Not when it's never been easier to learn in the history of the world!

With ever evolving content, the time has never been better to self-teach. In this fast moving world, things change on a weekly basis. If you're not up on the latest learning trends, then you'll be left behind in the dust as others rush forward.

New technologies arise all the time. Until traditional learning offers teaching to a new trend or technology, then it is already outdated.

Traditional learning is also very expensive. And what good does that do you if when you graduate and get out into the workforce only to find that you've still got a lot of learning to do since technologies have changed while you were holed up in the brick and mortar school?

With how slow traditional learning is, how is it even feasible to take these classes then try to get a job when things move so fast in the today's world? Once you get out of that slow moving class, you get out to find you only have more to learn. Now you're out money and time, both of which you will never see again as you try to play catch up with the rest of the world.

And what about the one size fits all teaching methods that don't work for you? What about what's most suitable and an effect method for you? Don't you deserve to get to learn in the way you do best?

When you learn by doing, it's faster and teaches you exactly what you need to know and in the fastest way possible. I'm sure you've looked at college curriculums before and wondered why you would need some of the classes listed on it for the degree you would like to get. The extra classes cost you extra money, time, and most importantly brain space.

Why try to fit in something that has nothing to do with what you need to know? Why pay for something that you won't need to know? Why waste your valuable time on something you won't ever need to know?

There's absolutely no reason to do any of these things. There's no reason for you to miss out at all.

So, let's not wait any longer and let's get going on this adventure in learning!

But first, let's do a few exercises to help you better understand the differences in traditional learning and self-taught learning.

In self learning, you can learn on your own time?

    (a)   True
    (b)   False

In traditional learning, you can learn on your own time?

    (a)   True
    (b)   False

Teachers in traditional classrooms have access to cutting edge technology and teach their students about these new ideas and ways of doing things?

(a)   True

(b)   False

If you are in a traditional college and want to earn a degree in Physics, will you graduate and be ready to step right into a job in your field?

(a)   Yes

(b)   No

(c)   Probably not

Chapter 2

Principles of Self-learning

'Learning never exhausts the mind.' - Leonardo da Vinci

Now that you've decided to become a self-learner, you must understand what it means to be both the student and the teacher. It's not easy, so I'm not going to lie to you and tell you it's a piece of cake.

The first thing you've got to master is time. There are only twenty-four hours in each day - seven days in a week – fifty-two weeks in a year and you have no idea how many years you will have on this Earth. So budgeting your time is an essential skill.

Time-management will be the first thing that you have to learn. You can do this by making yourself an hourly calendar, much like an appointment calendar. You will give yourself the amount of time you feel you will need to complete each learning task. You will have to adjust these times to fit what you will actually need after you get started.

Making sure to schedule your days, the times in those days that you will devote to learning and giving yourself breaks will be the foundation of your self-learning endeavour. Don't take this step lightly. As with the foundation of anything durable and long-lasting, you will want this to be strong enough to withstand time.

The time-management skills I learned when I began my online college classes still serve me today, with my writing career. I have worked with others who have never mastered the art of time-management. To say it was bothersome to work with them is an understatement. Those who have no idea how to properly manage their time have little output. And when working with others, it's important to understand what their time means to them. So, please set up your time appropriately before you even begin to start your learning process.

Now, you will want to use the MASTER principle to teach yourself. People who want to try accelerated learning use this principle. You will want to use accelerated learning as well, so you can get the most out of your time.

The first word in this MASTER principle is Mindset. As you can imagine with a task as big as self-teaching, your mindset it of the utmost importance. If you go into this with a sour attitude, then you will not succeed. But if you go into this with enthusiasm, your eyes wide open, knowing that this will be hard work which will require you to have self-discipline, then you are starting off on the right foot.

Again, back to time-management, adhere to your schedule. If you put on your schedule that you will begin learning at nine in the morning, do just that. Don't put it off until nine-fifteen. Don't think that starting at nine means putting the coffee on at that time. Be sitting down, ready to get to work and have the right mindset to get things done by that time.

Along with time-management, mindset is the key to success. If you get these two things down, the rest is a gravy train.

The next thing in the MASTER principle is the acquisition of knowledge. This sounds silly as of course, your next step after setting your mind to work is acquiring knowledge, but it has to be said. You've got a job to do, and acquiring knowledge is it.

But where to find that knowledge is another question. The third letter in MASTER is 'S' seeking or searching for the material and the meaning of what you need is next.

Do you find a book? Do you look online? Do you have to go outside of your normal place of study to find what you need? Knowing where to find the things you will need to gain this knowledge you want is important and there are many places to find it. You've just got to narrow it down to where that is.

Once you've got the information about where you need to seek this knowledge, you need to see what's stored in your memory banks about this topic. Triggering your memory may help you to speed up this learning process for this particular task.

In accelerated learning, a way you will want to learn to save you time and maybe even money, you will use every available resource to gain new concepts, ideas, and knowledge on your given subject. If you happen to have a little information stored inside of your head, jot that down. You might as well use what you've accumulated in your lifetime to help you get ahead of the game.

Once you've got all your studying done, you will want to exhibit that newly acquired knowledge. Exhibiting your knowledge can be done in lots of different ways. You might make a paper, a video, a slide show, or even a lecture on what you've learned.

The important thing is to have something that shows what you've learned, even if you don't have any plans on showing it to anyone, you should have it ready as if you did. One never knows when one might be called upon to help another understand what you've come to. It's not only nice to help others understand and learn what you have, but it helps you to cement that knowledge into your brain in a way that nothing else can.

Plus, if you have this information down in some type of a format, you can go back and use this if you come across another idea or task that involves this knowledge. You won't have to reread or re-learn things about this subject if you have put down somewhere what you already know.

Being the student and the teacher is fun, innovative, and most of all, rewarding. This makes you a better student than you ever were before. And it also brings out the teacher inside of you that you never knew was there.

How nice will it be to not only gain knowledge and understanding of things you never thought possible, but to be able to teach yourself and others too? Well, who would've ever thought you could do such a great thing?

And to know that you've always had it in you too is another thing that intrigues the mind. Knowing that we all have it in us to become our own teachers is kind of mind-boggling.

With just a few bits of helpful advice, you've always had the makings to become your own teacher. Learning something as simple as the MASTER principle not only enables you to teach yourself but to do so in an accelerated fashion. And you can do that for others too if you ever need to.

Motivation is all you will ever need to get going on this dream of a lifetime of unlimited knowledge and understanding. Motivate yourself to learn more. Motivate yourself to make every single day an important day for you, a day where you will learn at least a little something new.

It doesn't matter if what you learn isn't life-changing. Just learning little things adds up to life-changing eventually. Think about how the television shows have grown more and more educational. There are shows about all kinds of things that we never had before.

With all the science shows out there, all of us have a lot more knowledge about scientific discoveries, ideas, and even origins of our planet and the things on this planet. Our world has gotten smaller, at least when it comes to being able to learn all about it, without having to travel the globe.

I'm glad we don't have to travel to Africa to find out how the lions live their lives. And I had no idea I even wanted to know about that. After stumbling onto a television show about African lions, I found myself not only engaged in the video, but getting on my computer to find more information out about the animals.

Along with finding out about the lions, I also found out about the tsetse fly. These flies bite and suck blood. They can also transmit deadly diseases and some people even die from what they catch from the bite of one of these insects.

Sure, am glad I've got sources to help me learn about things I wouldn't ever learn about if I had to travel to regions with flies that can kill you!

What about other places that we could never go unless we'd been highly trained? What about the deep, dark depths of the oceans? What about the dark recesses of outer space?

If it weren't for technology and the rapid way information can now be distributed online, we would have to go to college for years to become an astronaut. And even if we were able to get all that training, it wouldn't mean our physical bodies would allow us to travel to space.

So, let's talk about physical limitations for a moment. These types of things can get in a person's way to get to schools and colleges. And even if you could get to these places, are the accommodations that great? Wouldn't it be easier, more comfortable to do your own learning at your own speed, and in the comfort of your own home?

My physical limitations might sound silly to some. I had kids in school that kept me from being able to drive two hours out of town each day to attend classes. Physically, I could not be in two places at the same time.

You know what I could do, though? I could do my learning online at home. I could take my laptop and do my learning in the car while I waited for school to get out. I could take that laptop to various sports practices that my kids had and not miss a single minute of learning. I could still be present in my children's lives and do for me too. I've got to admit that I never thought I'd be able to do that.

Being stuck in traffic as you've got to get somewhere can be frustrating. But, if you've got some unexpected time on your hands and your laptop handy, you've got time to learn. Time has never been more well-spent.

All you need to do is get organized. Set those goals, make them realistic, and organize your time, your supplies, yourself and you're ready to get going on this.

Now, let's do a few exercises to see what we got from all this, shall we?

MASTER is a principle for what?

(a)   Having the right mindset before starting on a task.
(b)   Acquiring knowledge about that task.
(c)   Seeking material that has the information on that subject.
(d)   Using our own memories to help get the needed information on the task.
(e)   Exhibiting the knowledge we've gained.
(f)   Everything above

Why is mindset important before beginning anything worthwhile?

In time-management if you have to write a paper on biophysics that is ten-thousand words long? How would you fit this into your schedule?

(a)   I would understand that it would take three hours to find the material I would need for this paper.

(b)   I would understand that it would take me two whole days to write this paper of ten-thousand words.

(c)   I would give myself time periods to rest.

(d)   I would do all of the above to make sure I used my time to the best of my advantage and turned in my paper on time.

If you master time-management without mastering mindset, will you still be successful?

(a)   Sure

(b)   No way

MASTER principle is not only used in self-teaching but in what else?

(a)   Teaching dogs tricks

(b)   Cooking

(c)   Writing a book

(d)   Learning new things in a faster way.

(e)   All of these.

Is it easier to be a student with a separate teacher? Or is it easier to be both the student and the teacher? And why?

Make sure to discuss these questions with yourself and maybe others to gain a better perspective of what I'm talking about in this chapter.

Chapter 3

Align Yourself for Success

'You're never too old to start learning, and you're never too young to aim high and achieve great things.' - Asa Hutchinson

As a self-learner, only *you* can direct your education. If you want to do this all on your own, then you've got some things to do first. And a large part of it is getting to know what it means to be both teacher and student.

Teachers are given a curriculum from which to teach. This curriculum is made by others who've studied extensively to understand what the students need to learn that particular year. And even before that occurs, others on a state level have mandated what the students in each grade are to be taught each year.

You've got a lot of work to do if you want to get on their level. Or do you?

The thing is, *you're* not trying to find out what thousands of children need, you're only trying to find out what *you* need. Only you know what type of learning you want.

So, you must do first things first. Like put down in words what it is you want to learn. Put down in words what time-frame you'd like to learn these things in. And then, you must put down in words how you will gain this knowledge.

Not everything is written, televised, or on audio. Some things have to be seen, in real life. If you've got that type of an agenda, then you must have that in writing to remind yourself of what all you must do to accomplish your goal.

Learning each new thing is one of your goals. You must have goals in place to reach the main goal of learning the subject matter you're after. And this brings us back to the subject of self-teaching.

You might recall that back in grade school, the teachers motivated you. Well, you won't have a cheering section, trying to get you all amped up to get some knowledge either. As a matter of fact, you might have people who actively get in your way.

One of the things I had to deal with were family members who thought I had free time since I was *just* doing school at home. I didn't have time, nor did I want to run their errands as they went off to work or school themselves. So, making people understand that you've got important things to do is a necessity.

What about knowing how you learn best? Is there going to be anyone who points that stuff out to you? No, there won't be.

You'll have to either understand the kind of learner you are, or you'll have to find a test online that will help you figure that out. What I'm getting at, is that you're on your own with this.

As daunting as that sounds, let's think about the good part of this thing.

You won't have someone telling you that you've got to learn something that doesn't pertain to what you really want to know. You won't have someone trying to cheer you on, when all you want to do is get to the task at hand. And you won't have to do things on someone else's time.

Your time will be your own. What you learn will be only what you want to learn. And you will be able to do it at the speed you want to. All you will need is the skillset to get things done. And with my help, you'll have that skillset.

I want you to get motivated to get this new learning thing going. I want you to start by thinking what it is that you really want to do and learn to do. Make a list if you need to. Look things up if you'd like. The sky is the limit.

You want to start an alpaca farm, start putting things on a list to get that going. You want to open your own bait shop but haven't fished a day in your life? Then you should start gaining all the knowledge you can on that subject so your bait shop can be a successful endeavor.

When I began to yearn for more in my life, I really had no clue what I wanted. I'd been a wife and mother for longer than I'd been anything else. So, I went for what was trending, making the money at that time. I signed up for Medical Billing and Coding. And guess what I found out? I hated it.

But I'd paid for the classes, so I finished them and got an Associate's degree. Then I went for Business Administration. Now, that I liked. I loved the classes and made great grades, learned a lot, then got a job as a property manager soon after graduation.

Guess what?

I hated being a property manager. So I applied for other managerial positions. And I didn't get any of those jobs, due to my age, though no one would admit that. No, they said I lacked experience. And I did. But I had this Bachelor's Degree that I thought made up for the lack of experience. I had a high GPA on top of that degree. So, why not give me a chance to prove I could do the job?

I'll tell you why. I wasn't going to be in it for the long haul. I wasn't in my twenties and needed to make lots of money to buy a house, a car, put food on the table for a growing family. No, I already owned a home with my husband. We had cars already too. And our children were getting out of school, getting their own jobs, making it so we didn't have to pay as much for them. In short, from an employer's perspective, I wasn't going to be hungry enough to do whatever it took to keep my job. I was a flight risk, due to my age and what I'd already accomplished.

And I couldn't argue that point either. If I didn't like the job, I could quit if I wanted to. But I wanted to work. I wanted to use my brain for more than just figuring out what I'd make for dinner, or what type of laundry soap smelled the best.

So, I further educated myself in a non-traditional manner. I started learning how to write and what to write about. I'd learned time-management and knew how to gauge my turnaround time for writing projects.

Using my memories, triggering them, I was able to use what I knew to move forward and learn more. And little by little, I kept learning and getting further and further ahead. And as far as I'm concerned, I'll never stop learning and moving forward.

But that was me, how about you?

What is it that you've thought about doing that you just thought wasn't within your grasp? What makes you think? What makes you smile? What motivates you?

I wrote articles when I first started my writing career. And as far as I knew when I'd begun doing that, I would only do that from then on. But one day I picked up this book. A very popular book that had world-wide readers. It was so popular two more books were written, keeping the odd love story going. And then even a set of movies came out. And all the while as I read and watched, I thought to myself, I can do better than this.

I thought I could make at least one better book than that trilogy. And you know what, I did. But I made more than one great book that made the best sellers lists. I made lots and lots of them.

But I didn't go about doing that the traditional way either. I had to go around the old ways and try new ways. I had to think outside the box. In the end, I got more than I ever dreamt I would. It didn't matter to me that my name wasn't going to go down in the history books either. The only thing that mattered to me was that I'd set out on an adventure and I'd had it and been successful at it along the way.

So, think about that when you're coming up with what it is you'd like to tackle. Be ready to take roads less traveled. Be ready to make adjustments to your goals. But keep moving toward those goals, even when you do adjust them.

Once you get your mindset going, you'll need to find your perfect learning environment. Not all of us can learn at the kitchen table. Maybe your house is a bit on the noisy side. You might want to find your learning spot at a local library, or a park, or a cafe. Wherever you can find that place where you can think without being bothered too much, just do it. Make that your personal learning environment.

Maybe you've got an old shed that you can convert into your own school room. Maybe your bedroom would be fine if you added some tapestries to the wall to help dampen the noise level. There are so many possible ways to improve your surroundings, the sky is the limit. And if that fails, leave and find the right place for you.

Next, I'd like you to think about target setting. It's important to set up a target point to start things. Maybe it'll be by next year or maybe sooner than that. Whatever it is, set it up. Make that target. If you don't make a target, then you won't have anything to set your sights on.

What about learning secrets?

Yeah, I've got a few for you. You have probably heard of speed reading. There are many classes offered to learn this technique. And you could pay for one if you wanted to. Or I can just give you the low down on what speed reading really is.

In any sentence there are words that matter, content words and there are words that don't really matter that much, function words. You can skim over the words, picking out the content words and get the idea of the writing.

Here's an example:

Sherry will be doing the dishes tonight after dinner.

Here are the words that matter, the content words: Sherry, dishes, tonight.

The rest of the words only serve to make the sentence a bit more informative. You can imagine someone saying, 'Sherry. Dishes. Tonight.' Chances are that you would understand that the person saying the words wants Sherry to do the dishes that night. Who cares when it is, after dinner? Who cares about the words, will be doing the? All we need to know are the three content words. And after some practice, you will be able to pick out the most important words in each sentence and skim over the rest, making you a speed reader.

You should know that you will have to go back and re-read some things, even after you get good at speed reading. At times, things can distract us and it's important to make sure we've got all the important stuff in our brains. Going back to read over things isn't a bad thing and it doesn't mean you've failed speed reading. It's all just a process anyway.

You will also want to know the art of smart note taking. When reading about things, watching things that will help you learn, or listening to things, you will want to jot down the important parts of that.

As with speed reading, jotting down the content words will help you a lot more than trying to transcribe word for word what a speaker is saying or how a passage is worded.

Here's an example of smart note taking when reading a passage:

In the blue spectrum, there are three molecules that reflect light and two that don't. Molecules a and d do not reflect light, therefore they have no bearing on the subject at hand. While molecules b, c, and e do reflect light, making them the most important.

The smartest way to note this passage is: Molecules b, c, and e reflect light in the blue spectrum.

You've gotten rid of a ton of words and narrowed them down to the ones that really matter. That's what smart note taking is all about; getting rid of the words that don't matter, so that you can focus on what does.

You will definitely need to learn to memorize things in a fast way that keeps those things in your brain. When it comes to memorizing, it's all up to how you best recall things.

With our brains memorizing things in different ways, it's no wonder we need to know how each way works.

Sensory register is one way the brain memorizes. This means that you take in things with your senses. And what are your senses?

Smell, touch, taste, sight, and sound are your five senses. You can take in information with each sense.

Another way to memorize is through your working memory. This type of memory may not last long but it can get you through until you are able to jot down the information.

The method of Loci is one way to memorize. Loci is Latin for places. I bet you've already got a good idea of how this technique works.

Visualization is key to this technique. You will visualize a place, such as your school. You want to remember where your English class is. There are three hallways when you enter the building. So, the building is the place you will recall first. Then you will see yourself in the entrance, taking the hallway that leads to your English class.

Another technique is the Mnemonic Peg System also know as the phonetic number system. This is where you put together a list and number the items on it. One – let the dog out each morning. Two – put the dog's food in his bowl and place it on the same spot on the floor each day so he can find it. Three – leave the doggy door unblocked, so he can get out to use the bathroom while you're gone. Four- if you forget any of these steps, your dog will go hungry and use the bathroom in your home. Now, this is stored in your long-term memory.

So, here are the essential keys to help you align yourself for success and here are a few exercises to help you too.

Does your mindset really matter if you're to become successful?

(a)   It surely does
(b)   Nope

Is time-management a waste of time or not?

(a)   I don't see the use in learning time-management. When I have time, I'll get to it.
(b)   If I want to get things done, then I need to make up a schedule that will help me.

The Loci method of memorization uses _______to memorize things.

(a)   Words
(b)   Ideas
(c)   Thoughts
(d)   places

The Mnemonic Peg System uses _________ to memorize things.

(a)   Watches
(b)   Times
(c)   Numbers
(d)   faces

Chapter 4

Find Your WHY

'Live as if you were to die tomorrow. Learn as if you were to live forever.' – *Mahatma Gandhi*

As people, we have a few needs which are basic and need to be met before we can even hope to move forward. The need for security is one of those basic needs we all have.

We also must have a need for identity. Who am I really? Who do I want to be? Who will I become?

Stimulation is another of our most basic needs. We are born with the need to be stimulated. Some babies need to be stimulated in order to eat. And all babies need visual stimulation as well as verbal and touch.

Once these basic needs are met, we can move forward.

Motivation. What does that word mean to you?

Are you easily motivated? Is it hard to get yourself motivated? Do you rely on others to motivate you?

If you are going to be a self-learner, you must learn how to motivate yourself. Being all on your own, means having to do all things on your own. You can't count on anyone to motivate you.

First, let's learn a little bit about motivation. There are two types of motivation. When motivation is generated internally, this is called intrinsic motivation. This is the type of thing that gives you joy or you feel like it's your job and enjoy doing a great job, even if it is just for yourself. Think about how you take pleasure and pride in keeping up your appearance, if you do that kind of thing. Doing your hair motivates you in a way that keeps you excited and on track. You wouldn't ever think of doing your hair then just stopping there. No way! After that is makeup, then finding just the right outfit and what about shoes?

You didn't do all that just to please anyone else. Sure, you like the compliments, but you're main goal was to like what you see in the mirror. Everything else is just extra frosting on an already delicious cake as far as you're concerned.

Now let's talk about another kind of motivation. This type of motivation comes from the outside world. People who tell you that you look pretty today even though you didn't do anything to yourself to make yourself look any better than you do any other day. This could motivate you to start a beauty regiment. Extrinsic motivation comes for others. You won't get this type of motivation very often when you are self-learning.

But one never knows for sure nowadays where you will get motivation from. Some of you have jobs that will have managers who are trained to motivate you to do some self-learning on your own time and maybe even on the company's time as well. It's important to take whatever time is given to you to learn. Even if your head's not in it right away, you never know when something on the internet might motivate you.

Here are some things you can do to help with self-motivation:

Seeking and seizing opportunities that intrigue you. Going the extra mile to achieve goals set by you and others will help you learn how to get motivated and stay that way. Looking for ways to improve by asking for feedback is also a great way to motivate yourself into doing the best job possible. And setting realistic goals that are still high is a great idea to keep yourself motivated.

But what about setbacks? Will those send you into a tailspin?

You can't let things that don't go right get in your way. Sure, you can give yourself a speck of time to experience disappointment, but don't dwell on it. Just pick yourself up, dust yourself off, and start all over again.

If you liked what you were doing in the first place, then doing it over again ought to be just as much fun. And even more fun since you've got the basics down and are just adding in some more glitter to make it all really spark this time around.

So, you've got that motivation going strong as you move forward, taking strides toward that goal you've set for yourself. It's up there, but you know you can get to it.

How do you keep up that level of motivation?

Staying positive helps a lot. Don't let niggling worries get to you. You *will* make the deadline. And if you can't do that, then you *will* come as close to it as you can. You won't let that get in your way. You *will* keep thinking positive, no matter what.

Don't lie to yourself about what your weaknesses are. And know your strengths too. If you know you've got a tendency to need a nap around two in the afternoon and for some strange reason have scheduled yourself to work right through that hour, then change it. Don't put yourself into binds if you don't absolutely have to. Schedule your nap for that hour, instead.

Your strengths are to be noted too. So, you do your best work from nine in the morning until eleven. Great that you know and understand that about yourself. Why not schedule the hardest part of your task for that time? It makes perfect sense, doesn't it? And it will keep you motivated to keep on going with your project.

Know the company that you keep. If you want to stay positive and upbeat about not only what you've got going on but what others have happening in their lives as well, then you need to have positive people around you.

 No Negative Nelly's around you, no sir. Once in a while, those people can show up in your circle. You don't have to be rude, but you don't have to entertain their negative thoughts either. You're busy with loads of other things anyway. Politely excusing yourself to get back to work isn't mean, or inconsiderate at all and it gets you away from that negative energy so you can maintain your positive energy.

Don't be fooled, negative energy can be like a vampire, sucking your positivity away. Do your best to steer clear of that if at all possible. It can take that motivation you've had and send it to a place it can be hard to find again.

While you're at it, keeping that motivation going, keep on exploring new information. Keep on researching, learning, finding out new things. With this fast-paced world, new things pop up almost on the hour.

If you've got something to do, then do it. Procrastination is a thing of evil. Keep it at bay at all costs. This little demon can derail even the most thought out plans and highly motivated individuals.

Lastly, don't forget that asking for help is more than okay. Thankfully, you don't even have to rely on who's around you to ask for help. You can ask people online, from all over the world for their help and advice. And they're ready to give it too.

By the same token, you should share what you know with others too. When you've got some spare time, you can join clubs and organizations with like-minded people as yourself to exchange ideas and offer advice and help to those who need it. That, alone, can be a big source of motivation.

When you decide what goal you are setting, you need to make a commitment to that goal. You need to commit to seeing it through to the end, even if you do have things that get in your way.

Be ready to accept accountability for your project. Good or bad, you need to own it. Own your ideas, your drive, and even the downfalls. Own it all. It's not only good character, it's good for you to understand that people will hold you accountable for your endeavors. That will help you make your future goals.

Everyone knows that you will have to practice affirmation. We all need that pep talk at times and there isn't always someone around to give it to us. I'm reminded of a comedy sketch I saw once many years ago. But as funny as it was back then, it makes perfect sense for today.

Looking into a mirror, you can tell yourself what you think is a positive about you that you admire. Such as, 'I am a creative thinker.' I tell myself that all the time. Especially when people look at me like I'm nuts because I spout some book idea that's just come to me and have to grab a napkin or any other paper product to jot down the essentials in the idea.

So what do you think is good about you? If you have to write down these things, then do it. Read them when you're getting a little low and know that these are truths about you that you are well aware of. You are special. You are unique. And the world is a better place for you being here.

As we go on through life, we want to grow. No one wants to stagnate. That's not true, we all know those people who don't care a bit about learning what's new. They won't get a computer to save their life. They don't want cable television as it's all just too much. They like things simple, like the way they used to be.

Good luck having a decent life with ideals like that.

I'm all for keeping things simple, but that doesn't mean cutting out technology. As a matter of fact, things have never been so simple in our complete past history.

No longer do we have to wonder what's going on in Russia. If we really want to know, all we've got to do is check out the internet. Heck, we could even find a social network friend if we're really curious.

Gone are the days of pen pals. We can talk to anyone we want all over the world in the blink if an eye. And thanks to online translators, we can understand them with ease and they can understand us too. This is a bright new world we live in, might as well use what we have to work with to our advantage.

When I was a young teen, I took my first computer class. There was no internet yet. You couldn't ask the computer to do anything as there was no voice activation. But I saw that it would be there someday. I saw, in that white box on top of my desk, the future.

I just knew that one day I would be able to find all the answers to any question that popped into my head in that box. And I was right too. What I didn't know was how all encompassing that box would become to me and most others on our planet.

With the technology we have, that alone should be enough to motivate you into learning more, doing more, living more, and helping others more.

Developing the mindset that you want to grow, learn, help is important. But don't just develop it and then let it sit there. Use that positive mindset to make things happen. It's not worth it if you don't use it.

And now for the hardest part of this whole self-learning thing. DISCIPLINE.

If you don't have self-discipline, then you will never get your feet off the ground. You've got to get up when you say you're going to get up. You've got to finish that reading by the time you said you would. You've got to get up off that couch to go outside and put those things together when you said you would.

Rome wasn't built in a day, and no one expects you to get that project off the ground and up and running in a day either. But you are expected to discipline yourself so that one day that project does see the light of day.

You deserve to see it through, don't you?

Getting yourself into the frame of mind to create self-discipline can be hard. My advice is to take it a step at a time. That's what I did.

I would drop my kids off at school, come home, start a load of laundry, eat some toast and eggs, then take a nap. I took a nap because I lacked motivation to do anything else.

So, how did I pull myself out of that go-nowhere routine when I still had no idea of what I really wanted to do?

I started going outside after breakfast. I got on the lawnmower, I cleaned up the flower beds, I hoed weeds. And then, when the yard looked great, I went inside and began working on the house. I organized every closet in the house, then I did the same for the kitchen drawers, the fridge, the laundry room.

I'd motivated myself and I just kept going. I asked my husband what he thought about me doing online college, could we afford it? I wanted to learn in the free time I had. He said we'd have to cut some costs, but we could manage it. So, I started school.

I had my setbacks. I could've stopped. But I didn't. I kept going forward. I kept learning for free now. I kept looking for that opportunity to do more, learn more. And I found it.

You can too. You can do anything you set your mind to. I promise you that you have the power, the wherewithal, and the knowhow to get it done. All you've got to do is get motivated.

So, let's do some exercises to see what you've learned:

You have to be a college graduate before you can take any free online classes.

- (a)   Of course, you do.
- (b)   Why should you need a degree to take some free online classes? You don't need any type of degree at all to get some free knowledge.

If you lack motivation, you can succeed anyway. All you need is money to succeed.

- (A)   True
- (B)   False

If you keep friends around who are negative, you can still be the bright light in the bunch and they won't try to put your light out.

- (A)   True
- (B)   False

If you have a positive attitude and you hang out with others who have the same attitude, the sky's the limit.

- (A)   True
- (B)   False

If you fail once, you should just quit. You don't have what it takes anyway.

- (A)   True
- (B)   False

If you know something and someone asks for help with what you know, should you keep that information to yourself because you want to know more than anyone else?

- (A)   Yes, why let anyone know what you do? It gives you an edge they don't have.
- (B)   No, you should always share the things you know that might help others. There's plenty of knowledge to go around, no need to hoard it.

If you have an idea, make a goal, then gather the information to bring that goal to life, do you have to have motivation to carry it out?

(A)   No, all you need is the knowledge

(B)   Yes, you still have to have motivation to carry out all the steps that come with any goal.

Chapter 5

Manage Your Outcome

'Develop a passion for learning. If you do, you will never cease to grow.' – Anthony J. D'Angelo

In case you've missed getting the hint, *you* will be your own manager with self-learning. Getting the education *you* want, will all be up to *you*.

It will be you who chooses the right timeline to acquire this education. It will be you who plans out your week. It will be you who effectively uses techniques to help you learn better and faster. And it will be you who sets SMART goals to make sure you get what you're after.

And this is the most important thing – *you* will be the one to decide what the most important topics are that you'd like to focus on at one time. And you will also have to decide which topics that pertain to your main topic, that would be best left ignored.

And this is where I introduce you to the pareto principle. The 80/20 split. The theory is that for twenty percent of what's put in, one will have an output of eighty percent. In short, if you are given reading material of a couple of pages, this will give you enough input to make a report of forty percent more information than what you were initially given.

This is because we can take the smaller amounts of information and expand on them. Think of what it's like to have a conversation about something. One of the members of a group brings up a topic. That's about a sentence or two. Another person in the group adds a few more sentences to the topic. Now you've got the equivalent of one paragraph.

With this amount of information, you now have enough to make your own response, using what they gave. You can take that twenty percent and make eighty percent out of it. And you can do this because your brain can expand on what you've learned.

Let's talk about the advantages you have of being both the student and the teacher in one. Well, you know yourself. You know your strengths and weaknesses. You know what you like and dislike. You know what you want to know and don't' want to know. And best of all, you know how you learn best, be it auditory, visual, or hands-on. You know you, and anyone else who would take you on as a student would have to spend precious time learning all these things about you. So, you've just saved yourself a week's time just by knowing yourself. Congratulations!

The different techniques that come along with accelerated learning are things you can decide which to try and which to put to the side, knowing they aren't right for you.

The timeframe to get things done might be a thing a teacher would have done on her or his own time. Not you, you get to do things on the time that works best for you. Midnight session? Sure, why not? You're up, focused, ready to learn. Why not do it? No one else needs to be on your time, you don't need to be on anyone else's time, so take those midnight learning sessions if you'd like. This is your thing, your schedule, your time-management, do it your way.

Now, I've talked a lot about how you're on your own with this, and you are – mostly. But what I found when I ventured out on my own to write my first fiction novel was that there's this underground support system that you can only tap into when you're doing what they're doing. You know, like-minded people who are doing what you're doing or at least have done it. And it's cool because it's like members only. You don't have any onlookers who are judging you or saying negative things to bring you down. These clubs are to help lift you up and help you along the way they too are traveling.

It's such a great time to think outside of the box. There's so much more support for anyone who wants to do anything. Let's say that you'd like to learn about bread baking. You'd like to have your own little baking business but you don't know where to really start.

Here's the thing. Social media has all kinds of groups and clubs that you can join. All you need to do it post things about your interests. Make it known that you are a want-to-be baker. Then type in baking groups in the search area of your social media site and BAM! You're in, baby!

People are waiting for new arrivals to share their discoveries with. And soon, you will be there too, waiting, sharing, and living the dream. Connecting with people who are interested in the same things you are is a big help when you're on your own.

And talking about being on your own, you need to put a lot of thought into where you're going to do all this learning and achieving. You need some space to yourself.

I've seen walk-in closets made into writer's nooks. Walls adorned with pictures of their characters, the places they will travel to, the sounds of waterfalls echoing through the little area that make you feel as if you're on the tropical island with your characters. Things like this help you to get your mind into it.

Now, chances are that you don't want to become a fiction writer. It's not for everyone. But there is that thing you'd like to do and you need space to do it in. So make your own space. Let everyone in your household know that it's sacred to you and you will be forced to dismember anyone who dares to defile the sanctity of your private domain.

Get a dragon if you have to. Build a moat around your little nook of knowledge if you must. But get yourself some space and make sure you use it.

Let me just tell you now that trying to learn anything while sitting with your family, watching television, half-listening to your kids talk about what they ate for lunch in the school cafeteria and how it nearly killed them will get you nowhere. You need to use those time-management skills, I keep telling you to acquire, and you need to make time for family and only for them. By the same token, you need to make time to do what you need to do and only you need to do. Don't try to mix the two up. Don't try to multi-task this great effort.

Multi-tasking might work for some things but for learning, you must devote that time to learning, and nothing else. Your brain can only do one thing really great at a time. Multi-tasking is for things that don't take much brain power at all. But you need all your brain's power to learn fast and easily. Otherwise, you are defeating your purpose and wasting your valuable time.

At one point, I sat down and put a price on my time. When I did that, it made me realize that I had to get my time-management skills refined and ready to rock. Not long after refining my time, I was making money hand over fist, while still having time for my family.

Of course, you don't have to consider money. You can put it into something more valuable, like things learned. Like I said before, money can go away, knowledge never can. The point is to put regularity into what you do. Do it all on a regular basis, make it your routine to take time for the different things in your life that are important to you. Soon, you will see how things fall into place as if my magic.

Now let's look at ways to develop time-management skills. There is more than one way to break up time.

Take a method that was developed in the 80's. A man named Francesco Cirillo used a timer, like a kitchen timer to break time into sections. Mostly, he used twenty-five minute intervals and divided these with breaks of ten to fifteen minutes. This helped to make the time spent on working or learning not so monotonous. A large sector still uses this method to break up their days.

You might have heard of speed dating. This is where you get to talk to a person for only five minutes before the time is up and you must move on to the next potential love interest. What you might not know its that the same type of thing is done in the business world.

Speed networking is the equivalent of speed dating, in the end though, you might have more than one potential interest, only this interest would be a business one.

This type of time-management is called timeboxing. You put time into small boxes and use the time allowed only on the topic for that box. If you have six things to do in a week's time you might want to break them into this type of time-management.

In the timeboxing method, you would work on each of the six parts each day, giving the same allotted amount of time to each topic. At the end of the week, you've accomplished all you needed to get done on each topic while not burning yourself out if you would've done each one completely, one at a time.

I keep talking about the type of learner you are and how great it is that you might already know this about yourself, but I've yet to talk about what each type of learner is.

So, here it goes. There are three types of learners – yeah, I know I've said this a lot already. Here are the three types in big words, words you might use to research this subject – Visual, Auditive, Kinaesthetic are the three types of learning methods.

Let's start with visual. A visual learner uses vision to learn. Maps, pictures, different colors, as well as graphs and charts, and even reading material and writing help some people learn faster and better. This is the traditional way most people are taught in schools.

Next we have auditive. This one is simple, you learn best by listening to someone speaking about a topic. Plus, talking about the topic yourself helps you to understand it better.

Then we've got this big, long word, kinaesthetic. This is just a really big word for hands-on learning. Learning by touch, actually doing the task, helps some to learn a lot easier than by one of the other methods alone.

Now, this is just my opinion, but I like to use all three methods to learn things even quicker. This is called mixed forms. For instance, in what I do, writing fiction, it wouldn't do to just use visual learning to learn how to write a book. And auditive is great and all, but you need a bit more. Hands-on is imperative in the learning process too. So you might want to do as I did and use a bit of all three to learn effectively and quickly.

Let me also define target setting for you, just to be sure that you understand it completely, I don't want to leave you hanging, so to speak. First of all, you might hear or read this in two ways, target setting or goal setting. Either way, it means to develop a plan of action to motivate, and guide you to and through the goal or target. You know, make the end game, then make the plan on how to get there.

Now, let's make sure you understand SMART. This is an acronym that will help you set up your goals. S stands for Specific. It's important not to have something that's got too many vines going every which way. Be specific, have one thing you are going to get, by reaching this goal.

The M is for Measurable. You want to be able to measure things, be it in inches, time, or word count, make it measurable.

The A is for Attainable. Don't make your goal so far out that you cannot possibly attain it. Like, don't plan to go to the moon if you're not an astronaut nor have the capability to build yourself a rocket ship.

The R is for Relevant. Make it matter to you or to someone, don't make a goal that doesn't matter to anyone at all.

The T is for Timely. You don't want to spend years on a goal to make a doghouse. Make your goal timely. If you have a long-term goal, get to that goal by setting up short-term goals to achieve that one.

Getting your information from the best sources doesn't always mean that you automatically go to the library to check out books, or even go to the internet to surf the web. You might need to go actually speak to people, or attend events, or sign up for lessons of some kind. Whatever it is you need to do, do it, and don't look in one place for all of your information.

Be sure to keep in close contact with your peers. You never know when one of your group friends will stumble upon a gold mine of information that might just help you reach your goal.

Plus, you never know when one of your social friends will put out a call for help that you can help with. It's important to share your information with others when asked. That way, others will see how forthcoming you are and be that way with you too.

Believe me, it helps to have friends around the globe that you can turn to when in doubt. Getting the perspective of others from different backgrounds, countries, and even religions can be of great use to you when it comes down to it.

I once wrote a book that had an Irish character in it and some scenes from the Emerald Isle of Ireland itself. I would've had to do some massive research to find out the things a member of one of my social media groups gave me. Not only did it save me time, but it made my character much more believable. And when I read some of the book reviews, stating how realistic the Irishman in the story was, I felt pride in myself for having the forethought to ask if someone in that group might have some knowledge of Irishmen in the era I was writing in.

So, in short, having people to communicate with regularly is another one of the many keys that you will need to find the success you're looking for. You don't have to count on them to schedule your day, as a matter of fact, you *can't* count on them for that. But you can count on other's to help you figure out solutions to some of your problems. And you can count on them to give you their advice on how they met their goals or conquered their fears of going it alone.

You aren't the first person to take on self-learning, nor will you be the last. Let others help you when possible and help others when you can. Even though you're on your own with this, you're not all alone. Try to remember that when times get rough, and they will. Know that you can turn to either a group on social media or a group in your community to get the help you need.

Some social media groups meet in real life too. There are various large cities that have social media groups that also meet in person. In this way you can build an even bigger network of people to help you achieve your goals.

You can never have too much help when it comes to this self-learning thing. So much of what you will do will be on your own, take the time and the advantage of having others help you through hard times.

I can't tell you how many times I've gone to a group to look through the posts to find someone is about to throw in the towel, give up on their dream.

You can bet that all the positive responses those types of posts get, help that person to get back up, dust off, and try-try again. We all feel like giving up at times. It's only those who think the way we do, have the same interests we do that can keep us moving forward, without giving up.

For instance, if you are looking to achieve the goal of setting up a dog grooming business and you live with your wife and kids who do not like dogs at all. When you feel down, at your wits end, and about to give it all up, then you ask your family what they think you should do, chances are they'll tell you to give up.

They don't understand your need to see this goal to fruition after all. So, talk to people who know what you want, and also want the same things too. And don't put your heart out there to people, even well-meaning family members, about problems that seem insurmountable. The advice you get might be just the thing to end that goal you've been working so hard for.

We've covered a lot here, so how about we do a few exercises to see if we understand it all?

The Pareto principle refers to ________.

    (a)   The principle that parents are always right.

    (b)   The principle that says you can take in twenty percent and give out eighty percent.

    (c)   How a pig flies south in the winter

You can find likeminded people to communicate with about your interests where?

    (a)   Your next door neighbour's house

    (b)   The local mall

    (c)   Online and in person using social groups

When making goals, this method is the smartest ________

    (a)   The goal method

    (b)   The best method

    (c)   The SMART method

The time-management method of timeboxing is a lot like what?

    (a)   A boxing match

    (b)   Getting yourself into a box

    (c)   Doing things and putting them into boxes to ship out

    (d)   Speed dating and speed networking

There are three types of learners, these are ________

    (a)   Artistic, naturalistic, autoimmune

    (b)   Visual, Auditive, Kinaesthetic

(c)   Larry, Curly, Moe

Mixed Forms means _____

(a)   You mix different forms of learning methods to learn.

(b)   You mix different forms of letters to make a word

(c)   You mix concrete

An Auditive learner learns by _____

(a)   Reading

(b)   Writing

(c)   Listening

A Kinaesthetic learner learns by _____

(a)   Taste

(b)   Hearing

(c)   Touching

A Visual learner learns by _____

(a)   Talking

(b)   Walking

(c)   Reading, using charts and graphs, writing

Chapter 6

Effective Reading and Memorization

'There is no end to education. It is not that you read a book, pass an examination, and finish with education. The whole of life, from the moment you are born to the moment you die, is a process of learning.' - Jiddu Krishnamurti

The importance of reading and memorization aren't only keys to success, but they are the most important ones. When I talk about reading, I mean that the written word is important, but you can listen to these words too on audible devices. There is more than one way to read after all.

And there is more than one way to memorize. In this chapter, we'll go over the different ways of memorizing things. At least one of them will work for you.

There are various cool ways that you might have never thought about when memorizing things have come to mind. For instance, have you ever thought about the memories you now have and how you have kept them all these years?

What about the way Grandma's kitchen smelled each time you came to her house for a visit? Is it the smell of cinnamon from her famous homemade rolls that fill your nostrils with the sweet scent each time you remember her? Or maybe the smell of tea brewing on the stove that you can smell as if you were really there.

There's a name for that type of memory – Sensory memorization is the way one can recall things using one or more of the five sense.

And just a reminder of what our five senses are – smell, sight, touch, taste, and sound. Each one of these senses can trigger memories. So this means that you can make new memories using your senses too.

Now, let's go back to that memory of your grandmother. When you think about her, you smell cinnamon, right? What happens if you walk into a place and smell cinnamon?

I bet a lot of times, it makes you think of your grandmother. Cool, how it works both ways, huh.

Let's use another sense, shall we? How about the sense of sound?

Most children have memories of a certain song that was sung to them to help them go to sleep at times. When you recall this memory, you hear the song in your mind. You can recite all the words and feel the safe, warm, comfortable blanket you were wrapped in.

Let's change it around. You walk into the lobby of a hotel and hear a woman singing the same song to her baby to help it calm down in the unknown place. What happens to you then?

The same thing, huh?

You are taken back to that time and place where you too were sung that song. Here come the words to the song again, the same safe feeling, and you probably have a smile on your face too.

What about taste? Did you ever eat a hotdog on a hot July fourth afternoon? Now, this is a bad memory, but one to remember none the less. The warm summer afternoon, the hotdogs sat out too long and you ended up with food poisoning. Yuck!

Whenever you taste the same brand of chili you had on that hotdog, it takes you right back. The summer heat, the smell of the port-a-potty you found yourself in the majority of that afternoon after eating that hotdog that turned your celebration into a nightmare, it's all right there in your mind again.

Not only will you never eat hotdogs that have sat out any length of time at all now, you will never, ever eat that brand of chili again for the rest of your life. And you can thank that to sensory memory.

Remember that sunset that you and the person you first fell in love with sat hand in hand, watching the vibrant colors melt into the ocean? Bet most times you catch a glorious sunset with those colors, watching them over a body of water the way you did back then, you go right back there to that time and place. You go right back to that old feeling of finding yourself in love and how remarkable that whole thing felt.

How about touch, huh? That old blanket that you used to carry around when you were a kid? It was made out of terry cloth. There were patterns on it that you would trace with your finger. Then one day while at Bed, Bath, & Beyond, you find another blanket. It's got the same fabric, the same type of pattern. You run your finger over it and there it is, all those great memories of you and your blanket.

It's like you don't think of those kinds of things for years and years, then something comes up, it hits you in one of your five senses and off you go on a journey you never expected to go on at that moment in time.

I bet you've used your working memory before. This is a short-term memory. You won't hang onto this memory for long, unless something special happens to burrow it into your long-term memory bank.

When you use your working memory, you only need to keep it there until you can get the small amount of information written down or saved somewhere. When someone gives you their phone number and you're without any way to keep it. You might repeat it to yourself silently in your head or even out loud as you go to get something to write it down with.

Now this type or memory can turn long-term, as I said before. Let's say you jot that number down. Later on, you and the owner of that number do something amazing, you fall in love. Well, now that number is embedded in your memory.

You might even fall out of love after a while, chances are that phone number will crop up in your mind from time to time without you even trying to think about it. It's weird how our minds and memories work.

That long term memory, triggered by a major event in your life is the third way we memorize. You'll never forget your wedding day. Everything about it is there in your long-term memory. Even the short-term memory you had of keeping that phone number there in your mind until you could write it down.

So, there it is in a nutshell. The three memories are, sensory, working, and major events – even tragic ones.

Now that we know this, what can we do with it?

There are methods of memorizing things that use how me make memories and uses that knowledge to our advantage. The Loci method involves using places to make memories last.

You've got to learn a building, a new city, a grocery store. You use the Loci method to map it all out in your mind. Let's do a grocery store.

First of all, it's always a great idea to know your local grocery store's layout. That way, when they rearrange, you can complain and know that you're right about where certain things used to be. So, this type of memorizing will come in handy when you've got to re-memorize your local grocery store after a makeover.

You come into the store through the front doors, of course. There's the produce to your right, the registers to your left, and straight ahead is the flower department. Each aisle might have a sign above it, telling you what's down each one. You don't need no stinking signs, you've got Loci.

Zipping through the store, you do all of your shopping in record time. Not once did you have to go back and search out an item you missed. You are a master at grocery shopping and everything else you do, darling as you know about Loci and you use it to your advantage.

The Mnemonic Peg System is one you might of heard of before. It's the memorizing system that uses numbers or letters to keep items in check for storage.

Let's say you've got to do household chores. Now, you've only got one day to get everything done. You've made a list of what needs done. Number one, put the clothes on to wash. Number two, do the dishes. Number three, sweep the floors. Then you have to take a nap.

When you wake up, you dreamt of eating a marshmallow and find your note is gone. You've made the age-old mistake of eating your note. What can you do?

Stop doing the housework?

No way. You promised you'd get it all done. You wrote the note. You read the note. It's there, in your memory. All you've got to do is use that Mnemonic Peg System or Phonetic Number System, as it's also called, in your mind. Now, you can see it all there in your head. 1. Laundry 2. Dishes 3. Floors. And then what?

4. Beds 5. Windows 6. Ceiling fans. And now you're done.

Having a built in system can help you out of a jam.

Let's think about how our long-term memory works for a minute.

Have you ever been out somewhere when you saw someone? They wave, you stare, unblinking, unthinking, and immovable. Do you know them? Slowly, it comes to you that you've seen them before, but they're out of place.

Oh, yeah, it's Jones from accounting. You know him, you just have him stored in the office part of your memory.

What about places? You may not have been in a certain town for years, but you've still got memories of it. The tall water tower in the middle of town, the way main street had old fashioned stores along each side of the road.

Now if that little town had had a major overhaul, you're going to feel lost there. It won't be the same. But if your landmarks haven't changed, you will know where to turn to get to Cutty's bakery and get one heck of a great kolache.

And don't worry if something you thought you had stored in your memory bank is just gone, vanished. Periodically, your brain has to do some cleaning, make space for new stuff by getting rid of things you don't use much.

So if that dog's name you had in third grade goes missing, let it go, dude, move on. You'll fill that empty spot with something new before you know it. Spot? Yeah, that was his name. And there you've got it back, and now your brain must find something else to try to toss in the rubbish can.

What if you put something in a place that you make a point of remembering? You don't want anyone to find the remote to your television. You put it away in your top drawer and you look at the spot it's in, cradled there in the comfort of your black undies and your white socks.

Later, you go to your room to chill and watch some Netflix, but the remote isn't where you left it. You know you left it in the top drawer. You know it!

In a rage, you go through the house, threatening everyone with death unless the priceless remote is given back to you. No one will come clean about it. No one!

You don't want to reveal your clever hiding spot, so when asked where it was that you left it, you keep your lips sealed tight. No way you're letting that secret leak.

When someone tells you they did go into your room to put some clean laundry away, you run back to your room, pull the top drawer open and gently move away the top layer of underwear and socks. And there lies your precious remote and you are back to your normal, sane self once more. And all thanks to your keen memory.

Making memories isn't something we even think about doing, it just happens. You go to the same school for years, you memorize the names of the people you went to school with – friends or not – you know their name, face, and maybe a little something else about them. Like, that's Nancy. She was in a few on my classes. She ended up being the Valedictorian of our graduating class.

There are a couple of ways of learning that I'd like to hit on. You might remember hearing or reading something about Pavlov's dogs. He used food to help prove that we all have ways of learning certain things.

Before feeding the dogs, he would ring a bell. Shortly after the bell was rung, the food would be served to them. They were taught that with the sound of a bell, food soon followed. Which isn't always the case, but it proves that most anything or one can be taught to believe something, whether it's true or not.

This type of learning is called associative learning. This is, in short, the response to a stimulus.

A child may come to think that using the potty will get them a cookie if that's the stimulus used to get the correct response from the child using the potty. Later, they will find that in reality, no one is waiting there with a cookie when they use the bathroom. Bummer!

There is also passive and active learning. Passive learning is what has been done typically in classrooms. You sit, read, listen, watch, but you do not get up and you don't touch anything.

Active learning is just the opposite. You get up, you listen and you talk, you touch and you watch. You get active in the learning experience. This is known to make a lasting impression on people. When you actually do something, it becomes a memory, unlike when you read about it.

Think of any book you've ever read. While reading it, you were engrossed in the story, at one with the lead character. You cried when she lost her dog for Pete's sake. Three years later, you see the same book lying under a pile of dust beneath the book shelf. You can barely recall a thing about it. Why?

Because you only *read* about it, you didn't *experience* it in real life is why.

Have you ever heard of a memory palace?

Yeah, I hadn't either. But we all have them. Once, I went into a historic home. It was huge and we had a host who walked us through the place, telling us all about the history of the home.

Since I was there, actually experiencing it, not just reading about it, I have quite the memory of it all. I have a memory palace of it. Not only can I recall the rooms, the layout of the whole place, I can tell you what happened there too. I can tell you who lived there, died there, ate formal dinners there.

Almost as if I had once lived there, I have kept that memory. And there are other palaces in my mind as well as I am sure there are many in yours.

I went to California once. I ended up in Los Angeles and stayed on a beach. Every part of that trip is in a memory palace in my head. Stored away in a place I can go to and relive it all from time to time.

We've all got those old stories that help us remember things. Especially when you go to visit old relatives, the stories of the past come up. Old Uncle Eddie who died in the war of eighteen-twelve is always brought up. You never met him, but the stories are so vivid, you feel as if you had actually known the man who had eight kids, nine goats, and three wives long before you were even a twinkle in your father's eye.

We have so many things stored in our memory banks. It's hard to imagine we've got room for more of them. But we do. We have unending room. Learning can go on and on, without any fear of losing what's important up there in our brains.

With so many ways to learn, memorize, and move forward with learning, what kinds of opportunities are in store for us all? And how can we achieve them?

Not that long ago, people had their ability to learn capped at an early age. What they'd learned in high school, trade school, or college was it for them. Little else came their way in opportunities to learn things, live different lives, make different dreams come true. They had one job their entire lives. How boring!

It's nice to know we now have the ability to not do just one thing our entire life the way our parents, grandparents, and everyone who came before us did.

You've undoubtedly heard the stories of how your father graduated from Yale and became an attorney for the rest of his life. Yeah, sure he made excellent money. You all had wonderful things in life. But how much did he miss out on by only having one way to make a living?

Be thankful for this golden era of opportunity and use it. Be what they could never be. Be a top notch gardener even though no one in your family ever had a green thumb. That doesn't matter, now that you have all the education on growing vegetables you will ever need. You can win prizes with your green beans now!

So, what have we learned in this chapter anyway?

If you hear a bell, will you expect to be fed? Only if you are what?

(a)   A Russian cosmonaut

(b)   A spy

(c)   One of Pavlov's dogs

When you visit a place in your mind that is huge, full of memories of times, places, or big events, it's called a what?

(a)   Palatial estate

(b)   Splendid

(c)   Memory Palace

When you recall things using a list of letters or numbers it's called what kind of memorizing method?

(a)   Listing

(b)   Alphabetizing

(c)   Mnemonic peg system

Speaking of the Mnemonic peg system, what's another name for it?

(a)   Numbers, inc.

(b)   Pegs galore

(c)   Phonetic Number System

If you need to keep something in your mind for only long enough to write it down, what's that called?

(a)   Dashing memory

(b)   Quick memory

(c)   Hurry up or lose it memory

(d)   Working memory

Chapter 7

How to Constantly Get Better in Teaching You Anything

'People learn more on their own rather than being force fed.' – Socrates

Metacognition is a big word that means knowing how you think. When you think about the way you think, you are developing metacognition. Understanding how you decipher things is crucial in the learning process. Understanding how you learn best is also just as crucial.

Metacognition is important if you want to be both the teacher and the student. You must know how to best teach yourself. You must know how your mind works.

When you are on top and when you are too tired to learn is important, and when you use metacognition, you can determine these times a lot more accurately than anyone else can.

This brings to mind my old school days. I'm sure you have had days while in traditional schools where you just couldn't take anything in. You'd had a rough night and the morning classes just started too early for you to be able to concentrate on anything.

You have no control over when traditional schools start. You might not be at the top of your game at eight in the morning. That doesn't matter to traditional schools. Your first class starts then anyway. Do your best or you will fail.

You might even be great at that first period's subject, but you'll never know because it just comes to early for your brain to truly be awake and able to take in things well. How unfair is this practice?

You might have kids. If you do, then you know how hard it can be to get them up and going. They drag around, whining, whimpering, moaning. They don't want to eat yet. Their digestive systems aren't even ready to deal with the day yet.

For some of these kids, their mornings are starting at such early hours as four in the morning. They're shuttled from home to day-care and then on to school an hour or so later.

When you think about any homework or extracurricular activities they may have, you find they can't even begin to go to bed until maybe nine, ten, or eleven at night. How can anyone be expected to fully function on that kind of sleep deprivation?

Yet, it is expected of children as young as three and four-years-of-age. And we all sit back, scratch our heads and wonder why the children of America aren't keeping up with the children of the rest of the world.

It's simple, we are expecting too much out of people in general and the kids get lost in those expectations.

Let me give you just one family's weekly routine and you make the call yourself what is wrong with not only traditional schooling, but with the whole idea of what is good for kids in general.

There is a family of five. Mother and Father both work full time jobs. And sometimes their jobs even require overtime hours to be worked. These two parents have three children. One is in fourth grade, one is in second grade, and the other is in pre-k.

The parents both have to be at their jobs, that are an hour commute from their home, at six in the morning, each weekday. The children's schools don't even open until seven-thirty and classes begin at eight. This means the children must be woken up at four-thirty each morning to get dressed and make sure they have everything the will need for school that day. Then one of the parents drives them to their day-care, which has to open at three each morning to accommodate working parents and their children.

At the day-care, the kids try to sleep a little more but it's not always possible as other children are there, some crying, some upset, and some just plain grumpy from lack of sleep. A bit later, the school buses come to pick up the school-age children and take them to their schools.

Already, this sounds like a day straight out of hell to me. How about you?

Once at school, these three kids have to somehow get their minds right and get to their classes throughout the day. They must pay attention. They must try their best not to nod off in a boring class. And they must do well on their assignments and tests.

Once school gets out for the day, the get on a bus again to be taken back to the day-care as both parents are still at work. They wait at day-care until six in the evening to be picked up.

Does their day stop there?

No way.

The oldest has softball practice at seven. The second oldest has scouts at seven-thirty. And the youngest is in gymnastics at seven-thirty too. And this is only Monday. Tuesday they all have other things they do after school. Wednesday evening is church. Thursday is mandatory overtime for each parent. Friday there is finally nothing to do, and the whole family falls asleep in front of the television, fast food dinners in their laps left half-eaten at only seven in the evening.

Saturday starts early. The games they all had practice for during the week are going on all day long. Somehow they have to fit in doing laundry and cleaning house. Sunday they need to be at church then they visit family before going home to get ready for Monday. And then it all starts over again.

Unbearable. Unending. Unlikely that anyone will ever find that happiness that comes along with being able to do things on your own terms. Learn, on your own terms. Live, on your own terms. And all because this is how things are traditionally done.

Metacognition. Thinking about thinking. Understanding when you are at the lowest point of your game. Knowing when you are at the top of your game. Allowing yourself to rest. Allowing yourself to breathe. Allowing yourself to learn when you learn best.

Even if you have a job that takes up most of your time, you can make time to teach yourself things. You can take the time when you know you're ready to learn. When you're not distracted. When you're not tired. When you're not feeling down.

This brings up hard times on a person. Can you imagine how hard it must be to try to make yourself listen in class, to actually learn things when something bad has or is happening in your life?

There are sick days for work and school. But those days are limited. There are personal days at work, although also limited. What if you had the flu and used up all the time you had to be absent from school? What if you had no days left to be absent and something terrible happened?

Nothing so tragic that extenuating circumstances could be declared. Let's say your dog got hit by a car. It was taken to the vet but you had to go to school, you have no idea how it's going or if little Spot is still alive. How can you possibly do well in school on a day like that?

Metacognition allows you to think about how you would be thinking at a time like that. Your ability to learn that day would be shot and you would know that. You wouldn't waste time on even trying to learn on a day like that. But if you were in a traditional school, a place where not even one individual's circumstances can be put in the forefront. The day's work must go on. And if you're really lucky, you might get the chance to make up that test you failed because your mind just wasn't in it. But then again, that grade just might be put down in the gradebook and it will lower you average to the point that you will now need tutoring after school – adding that to your already insane daily schedule.

As daunting as all that is, thankfully there is a way not to live like that. There is a way to teach yourself on your own level and on your own time.

Now, let's talk about establishing habits.

You will need to get some good habits going. I go to bed at pretty much the same time each night. And before doing so, I get my house and chores wrapped up. I need eight hours of sleep each night, I know and understand that about myself and don't push to make myself deal with less hours.

Getting up each morning, I do the usual routine most people do to wake up fully. Shower, dress, make myself presentable. Then I eat a good breakfast before getting started on any learning or work.

Making sure that your mind isn't on anything else is a great idea if you want to be able to fully focus on what you've got planned for the day. So getting yourself ready for the day and filling your tummy with good food is important.

You're ready to get going on your work or what you want to learn that day. In the mornings, I work best. For this reason, I schedule myself to work until eleven-thirty. My mind is still on full throttle at this time, but it's beginning to burn a little too hot. It needs to cool down for a little while.

Making and eating a nice lunch, not heavy but not too light, helps me to chill for a bit. Drinking some water, maybe listening to music, I don't get back to work until I've given myself an hour to relax.

When I get back to work, it does take about a half hour to fully get going again. And this time I work until three. A fifteen minute break here, I eat some nuts or other light snack, drink more water then get back at it. Working until five, I get tons accomplished – either work related or learning related. In the end, I'm not exhausted. I'm stimulated, and feeling pretty light and free, even though I do have chores waiting for me.

The laundry needs done. There's dinner to make. And the family is coming home too. But with the way I scheduled my day, I don't feel overwhelmed at all. I feel at peace and actually enjoy the remainder or my evening. Along with that, I look forward to the next day.

I wish that for you too. And you can have that type of life if you use what I've given you here.

Now, just because everything I'm doing now is working for me, it does not mean that I won't have to improve my methods at times. Continuous improvement methods are available all the time. It's in my best interest to keep myself updated about these methods and put them into action to see if they help me or if they are of no help to me, or worse, a hindrance to me.

The thing is, that you need to try the new learning methods, memorizing methods, and any other methods you use, to see if they can improve things for you.

You might think you've got it all laid out so perfectly that nothing can make it any better. Well, I'm here to tell you that anything can be made better. Don't let yourself get stagnate. Do periodical research on methods and try them out. Even if you don't end up using any of them, you can tell others who might find them useful. The thing is to keep learning. Don't ever think you know it all, because there are always new things coming up.

 Lastly, I want to touch on the subject of Kaizen. The Japanese, notorious workers and learners, came up with this concept. Kaizen means to gradually make improvements and to do so continuously. This may sound too hard to do for you but it's not.

To implement Kaizen in your life, your work, and your learning regiment, you can start by taking small steps forward. With your life, think about your time, your diet, the things you do for fun. In work, think about how you can slowly adjust the way you do things to make them easier for you. And your learning regiment can always be improved upon. Maybe you will add in short trips to heighten your learning experience. Whatever you do, make it small so it doesn't upset your routine, only enhances it.

You should focus on actionable processes with kaizen. Nothing on the mental side alone, what you do should show. Also, getting rid of waste or excessiveness is part of this practice, which is ongoing, by the way.

Take action, don't wait and wait, just do it. Kaizen is about getting things done in a timely fashion. It's about making the way you do things flow easier, better, and faster.

In the end, use your own mental resources to help you make adjustments to your schedule and the way you do things. Think about how things could work better for you and others.

Look at your work community, your family, your own community as well. How can you take small steps to make them better? It can be as small as taking some time at home to make healthier meals for your family. Or it can be that you make sure to greet others at work with a smile. In the community, you might do something as small as picking up trash as you take your evening walks. Whatever it is, make sure it makes a real difference, and impact on people and things. Make it worth doing, even if it only takes a moment of your time to do it.

Using this idea, you can make great changes, a little bit at a time. Over time you will see a tremendous amount of difference and improvement in all sectors of your life if you follow this philosophy.

Don't we all want to make continuous improvements when we really think about it anyway? Don't we all want things to be easier as our lives go on? Don't we all want to make a difference in the people's lives who are around us, both at work, at home, and in our social lives outside of work and family?

Sure we do.

Life isn't just about us after all. It's about the world as a whole. A place where we can be ourselves while helping others. This is *our* world, *our* life, and *our* time to shine. And we've got this!

So, we're at the end of this chapter and it's time to reflect on what we've learned by doing some thinking exercises.

Metacognition means _______

(a)   You can move through space and time without using a spaceship.
(b)   You can use metadata to make decisions easier.
(c)   You can think about thinking.

When thinking about thinking, what can you do to help yourself?

(a)   You can figure out when your mind is at its sharpest.
(b)   You can find out when you like to eat ice cream.
(c)   You can remember who your high school crush was.

Establishing habits helps you do what?

(a)   Have more time to watch television.
(b)   Have more time to do what you want to.
(c)   Make your day more efficient.
(d)   All of the above

What kinds of habits are good ones?

(a)   Getting up at the same time each morning.
(b)   Eating breakfast each morning.

(c)   Buying new shoes each day at the same time.

(d)   Both a and b

By improving your methods continuously, you can ____

(a)   Build your own house.

(b)   Buy a new car without any money.

(c)   Find out new ways to do the things you already do.

Improving your methods on a continuous basis is smart.

(True)

(False)

Improving your methods all the time isn't practical.

(True)

(False)

If you want to be great, you find a way to do something and you stick with it. It doesn't matter if someone comes up with a better way to do it, you stay with what you've always done. That's the best idea.

(True)

(False)

Kaizen comes from what culture?

(A)   Iranian

(B)   Australian

(C)   Bohemian

(D)   Japanese

Kaizen is a philosophy or method that means you make small improvements all of the time.

(True)

(False)

 Making improvements, no matter how small, all the time is an impossible task.

(True)

(False)

Now for some questions you can think about.

What can you do to make your day a bit more efficient?

What can you do to manage your time better?

Do any of the time-management methods seem like they would work for you?

If so, which ones?

If not, why?

Do you feel like you can take the Kaizen philosophy and use it in your life?

If you make small improvements, what are the first ones you would make?

Do you feel that you can make an impact on not only your life by following some of the things you've learned in this book, but on other's lives as well?

And why or why not?

Conclusion

So there you have it. All you will ever need to get yourself started on the self-learning path. It's a path you will follow for the rest of your life. Once you get going, you'll find you never want to stop. It's addictive, in the best possible way.

Let's face it, everyone has some type of addiction, yours might as well be learning.

Armed with the tools you need to succeed, you can't sit back and wait any longer. Get up, get going, and get some knowledge. If it benefits you financially, great. If it benefits you in the fact that you know more, then awesome for you. Money isn't everything after all.

Knowledge is power, that much is true. Knowledge is worth more than gold. And knowledge never goes away like material things – that includes money - can do.

With what you have right here, you can get started today. Check out the free online courses that are available to everyone. Just take the chance and find something, anything to get that old brain a pumping again.

Oiling the machinery is always a good idea before starting up an engine that's been left untended for a while. Do yourself a favor and start out slow. Try something simple. Find that you can do it and try something a little harder next time. Whatever you do, don't stop. Keep going.

You've got your goals in place. Learn time-management. Look for an opportunity to expand your mind. Motivate yourself to get that learning done and done right.

You're all set. Now take a test online to see how you learn best, if you don't already know that about yourself. After that, you can look for all kinds of learning opportunities on the internet and beyond. Now that you know what kind of learner you are, the sky's the limit. Grab your pen, paper, computer, and some snacks for the journey and get going on it.

Why wait? Why procrastinate? Why not get started right away?

I don't care if it's something as trivial as playing a learning game on your cell phone. DO IT!!!

The key to this thing is to get started. Once you get going, it's like a roller coaster that keeps on moving, taking you on a wild ride you won't ever forget.

I can promise you that you will feel better about yourself when you are learning anything. You will have more confidence than you've ever had before. When you speak, people will listen. That's because you know things and they'd like to know them too.

Remember all that you've read here. Keep your notes close by. Do a little research on the things you've read about here. Make sure what I've told you is true. Second guess me, check my facts, do your homework on me and see if what I'm saying is true.

If nothing else, that has you on the right track. Don't take anyone's word for things. Check the facts yourself. In doing so, you create a tract for not only learning, but making sure that what you learn is real, good information, and not made up by some quack trying to make a buck. You can't trust anyone but yourself, remember that and always check the facts.

I know, crazy that I would have to tell you that, but in today's world, with technology being what it is, you can get a lot of fly-by-night scammers who like to prey on innocent people. Even if all they get is ninety-nine cents of your money, that adds up for them. The sad part is that it steals precious knowledge from you. What you thought you'd learned wasn't real at all and it goofed up your brain with fake facts that you'll have to unlearn, which isn't as easy as it sounds.

So, I end this book asking you what motivates you? What makes your brain light up? What makes you happy?

Now get to it and make yourself proud. You can do it!

Dear reader,

I sincerely hope that you feel inspired my book and enjoyed the Do-It-Yourself Exercises.

Before you close this book I´d like you to ask to write an honest review on amazon. It´d be greatly appreciated.

Just click here to leave a review on amazon.

Thank you and till soon!

Pat